Cricket as I see it

ALLAN BORDER

Cricket as I see it

ALLEN&UNWIN
SYDNEY • MELBOURNE • AUCKLAND • LONDON

First published in 2014

Copyright © Allan Border 2014

Allen & Unwin
83 Alexander Street
Crows Nest NSW 2065
Australia
Phone: (61 2) 8425 0100
Email: info@allenandunwin.com
Web: www.allenandunwin.com

Cataloguing-in-Publication details are available
from the National Library of Australia
www.trove.nla.gov.au

ISBN 978 1 76011 180 9

Set in 12/18 pt Sabon by Midland Typesetters, Australia
Printed and bound in Australia by Griffin Press

10 9 8 7 6 5 4 3 2 1

MIX
Paper from
responsible sources
FSC® C009448

The paper in this book is FSC® certified.
FSC® promotes environmentally responsible,
socially beneficial and economically viable
management of the world's forests.

I would like to dedicate this book to my family and friends, who've been rock solid through the good and bad times

Contents

Preface   ix

1 THE AUSTRALIAN WAY   1

2 CAPTAINCY   45

3 THE TWENTY20 REVOLUTION   75

4 THE MODERN GAME   93

5 BATTING   113

6 COACHING AND QUEENSLAND   147

7 TOURING   169

8 THE PATHWAY   197

9 POLITICS   211

10 THE GREATS   245

Epilogue   275

Looking back by Dene Border   279

Acknowledgements   297

About A.B.   299

Preface

I PLAYED MY last Test match for Australia 20 years ago, although it certainly doesn't feel like it was that long ago. It was 29 March 1994, South Africa versus Australia in the third Test of a series, a dull, boring draw during which I grew frustrated with the home team's tactics and then batted out the last day with that firmly in my mind, almost out of spite for the way South Africa had played its first innings. I made 42 not out in 225 minutes, and walked off the Kingsmead ground at Durban knowing it would be my last innings in a Test for my country.

I hadn't formally announced my retirement from international cricket, but I knew that this was the finish line, and I'll go into the story behind that in this book. I played a couple more one-day internationals on that tour, and I played two more seasons with Queensland in the Sheffield Shield and domestic one-day competitions before I stopped playing cricket entirely, thus beginning the cricketing afterlife.

Fortunately, it's been a busy time since then. When you are a professional cricketer, the game engulfs your life and the travel schedule is relentless, so filling that void is difficult for a lot of players, and I vowed to keep active and busy. I've been a national selector, in two stints, and I was on the board of Cricket Australia for several years, as well as several short stretches in cricket coaching. Currently I sit on the board of Cricket Queensland and the Brisbane Heat franchise that competes in the Big Bash League, and I'm a cricket commentator for Fox Sports, which keeps me active in the summer, and more recently I've also joined the ABC Radio team as an analyst.

The media work is my staple, and there's an irony in that, because as a player, I never, ever saw myself going into the media. As a matter of fact, I knocked back Channel Nine at the first approach 20 years ago, which may not have been my best decision! But I was uncomfortable with the idea I'd formulated that as a media commentator you had to be a strident critic. That wasn't for me; I didn't like the idea of jumping from one side of the fence to the other. But I realised over time that a commentator doesn't need to be potting players relentlessly, and that positive points can always be made. If criticism is justified, it's delivered.

Preface

It took me a long time to realise this, but I've now been with Fox for a decade or more and I really enjoy it.

When ABC Radio came asking, once again I was reluctant. My first thought was, 'How can you talk about cricket all day?' But the reality is different, because you do 30-minute brackets, and it's amazing how the anecdotes and circumstances bounce up around a cricket match when you put your mind to it. I've enjoyed working with the likes of Jim Maxwell, Drew Morphett, Geoff Lawson and the redoubtable Kerry O'Keeffe on air.

Coaching wasn't a career path for me. I took an under-19 Australian team away on a tour of Pakistan and went to a World Cup, but in truth I was an old-school type of coach, and at the time there was a move towards more modern coaching. To be brutally honest, I don't believe my communication skills were quite right to be a good cricket coach, and I recognised that fairly quickly.

My family has been a strong focus, and the four children my wife Jane brought into the world have had different views of me in a sense. Dene, our eldest, saw the tail end of my cricket career, but Nicole, our second, was young when I retired, and with the third and fourth, Tara and Lachlan, who never saw me play, I've made a conscious effort to be just Dad. I've been blessed with my family. Jane is a very capable individual and she's always had her own life, which is crucial. She's been a wonderful support for me, allowing me to earn my living from cricket. Nowadays Dene works as a currency trader with Macquarie Bank and lives in Singapore, playing some cricket, too. Nicole has completed a degree and works in public health, employed by the Cancer Council in Queensland. Tara, who has a media and communications degree, was successful in dance aerobics and works in that field, while Lachlan is studying exercise and sport science at university, and also playing some cricket. They're great kids.

When I stopped playing, I knew I'd need projects to drive me and occupy me, because I didn't want to become the stereotypical fat ex-cricketer, which is a constant battle. Early on I trained myself up and ran a half-marathon at Noosa, which was tough. It was a nice, flat track and a gorgeous day, and at about the 10-kilometre mark I was thinking, 'This is a walk in the park!' But at about 18 kilometres I started to feel the pinch, and an old guy ran up alongside me and commented, 'Only 4 k's to go!' My mind started ticking over; I was extrapolating how long it would take me, and I ended up shuffling the last few kilometres, groaning the whole way, literally. There were 80-year-olds bolting past me, but I did ultimately feel a sense of achievement. Nevertheless, I'm not about to go on the running circuit!

Trekking has become a passion for Jane and me, because we can do it together. We did Mont Blanc, the highest peak in the European Alps, which covers parts of

Preface

Switzerland, Italy and France, over 14 days, with every step a picture postcard. We also did a trek in Corsica off the south of France, and we've done some walking in Tasmania and the 223-kilometre Larapinta Trail in the Northern Territory. The Milford Track and the Routeburn Track in New Zealand also made a fun trip, and we threw in the coast-to-coast walk in England, from west to east. A few years ago I took Dene away and we walked the Kokoda Track in New Guinea along with the rugby league legend Mal Meninga and a few others with a group called Executive Excellence. That was a great experience. It was Dene's 21st birthday, and it was a wonderful father–son experience. Dene drew a sense of perspective from it, because there were boys younger than him who had fought and died at Kokoda. I see it as a really Australian thing to do, and it's no wonder that thousands walk that track every year.

Jane and I walked from Sydney to Brisbane for charity in 2002, raising more than a million dollars for children's cancer and juvenile diabetes charities. We took our inspiration from Ian Botham, who has done a few walks including John o'Groats to Land's End, the extremities of Scotland and England, and raised a lot of money for charity. It was an Ashes year, so Jane and I started at the Sydney Cricket Ground (SCG) and headed up the old Pacific Highway doing 30–40 kilometres a day, taking 31 days and arriving at the Gabba for the Australia versus England Test match.

We walked at a brisk pace, and we did some preparation. I also taped my toes and heels to make sure my feet would survive—it's not like wandering around a shopping centre for an hour or two.

Some of the people we had come along with us weren't so diligent, though, and Merv Hughes was a classic. When I rang Merv and asked him to walk with us for a couple of days, he was keen to do it, but I did warn him, 'Mate, do some training, and get some decent shoes and socks.' There was a pause, after which he offered, 'Mate, it's walking, isn't it? How hard can it be?' Well, Merv turned up with an old pair of Puma Sheffield cricket shoes, definitely not ideal for walking in, and socks that looked like he'd been using them since 1980! He immediately suffered blistering and aching shins, so he adjourned to the van after about an hour. On the second day he hung in bravely, but at the end of his stint he approached me with the shoes, held them up and said, 'A.B., can you sign these for me?' I said, 'That's a strange request, big fella, but yes.' As I was signing the shoes, he piped up, 'I'm going to hang them up next to my phone, and next time someone rings and asks me if I'll go for a walk, I'll look at these shoes, and tell 'em to get stuffed!'

These were projects I enjoyed, and that kept me occupied. But in the end, I'm a cricket person. That's who I am. I can sit there and watch cricket nonstop, whereas a lot of players switch off from the game, and don't like training or analysis. The game has never been a chore for me and I've never tired of it. I've kept track of it and still have things to say about it. That's why I've written this book, 20 years after my retirement. I hope you enjoy it.

Allan Border
July 2014

1

The Australian way

I'VE ALWAYS THOUGHT that Australians try to win games of cricket from the first ball. If they get into trouble, they try to save the game, whereas some teams start out trying not to lose, then go for the win if they're in the right position. That's a subtle difference in mindset, but it's important. I believe the aggressive game fits our national character.

We play better when we play aggressively, I'm absolutely convinced of that. There's always a line you shouldn't cross, and we probably cross it more than other teams, but I'd rather cop a black eye for that than play Mr Nice Guy.

On the Indian tour of 2013, when we lost badly, I felt sorry for the Australian players but there was an undercurrent in the way they went about the matches that bothered me. The pitches were very difficult for an

Australian cricketer, turning and dry from the start, and we don't see that type of surface much. They lost 4–0 so they deserved some criticism, but there was a split in the team and they weren't a happy camp. That can happen, too, but I felt we got away from the aggressive way we like to play. As to the pitches, we have to overcome that, because that's how teams will want to play against us now, particularly on the subcontinent.

You have to be thinking, 'How can we win this game?' Every decision you make, from the toss to the side you've picked, is about *winning the game*. It's about being positive with your cricket. I know other nations would try to debunk this theory, but I get the feeling that their decision-making is: 'Make sure we don't lose, and if we get into a winning position we go from there.'

I know that Australia can put up the shutters as well. Sometimes it's necessary, but it must only ever be a last resort. Up to that point, you should be conjuring ways to win the game. If you can't win, then of course do everything to save the match. And always put the team first in any decision-making.

I was a bat-first captain. I like the idea of getting runs on the board and then exerting pressure on the opposition to force them into mistakes, even on good surfaces. If you bowl good lines—good 'corridors', as we say—and keep that pressure up, you can bowl teams out. With a decent score on the board, you can retain attacking fields and not worry so much about stemming the flow of runs from the opposition. When you start bowling with no slips and have sweepers and all these defensive field positions, saving the boundaries, invariably the batsmen will dink the ball around and get five runs an over easily. That tactic just never works.

Sending in the opposition just wasn't my style. I think Ian Chappell advised me once: 'Nine times out of ten you bat first if you win the toss. The tenth time, you think about bowling first, but you bat anyway.' That thinking probably stems from the days of uncovered wickets, when you might be caught out on a sticky wicket and lose a game, so you needed to seize the advantage of batting first when possible. But these days you'd look at the opposition and the conditions. If I was playing India in Perth, I'd probably bowl first, but I didn't do that too often. In Brisbane and Perth, you can think about it because batting last isn't such an issue—the wickets tend not to break up there like they do elsewhere. But I imagine that the winning percentages over the history of Tests would be highly in favour of the team batting first.

If there's a declaration to be made to set up a match, you should set a big chase if possible. In days gone by, it was about dangling a carrot in front of the opposition, luring them into an unlikely run-chase that worked against them. But to my mind, you only do that if you're 1–0 or 2–0 down in a series and there might only be one or two Test matches to play, so you need them to go for it, and you need to give yourself more time than normal to get the 10 wickets. If you're 1–0 up in a series and you're batting in a strong position, why would you dangle a carrot?

What you do is bat to the point where history says they're highly unlikely to reach that mark. You could set an opposing side 400 in four sessions and potentially they could still win, but history shows you it's very unlikely. In the tied Test against India in 1986, I declared our second innings closed and set the Indians 348 to win on the last day, which was an example of the 'carrot' approach. But it was the first Test of a series, 350 to win is tough to get on a last day, and the wickets were going to be hard to extract. We almost won a famous match, and India almost made me regret that decision, reaching 347. It does happen that teams will chase you down. People still talk about Australia chasing 404 at Leeds in 1948, and who could forget the West Indians making a world-record fourth-innings 418 to beat Australia at Antigua in 2003, or Brian Lara's 153 not out steering the West Indies to a successful run-chase of 311 with a wicket to spare at Bridgetown in 1999? The point is, these are rarities.

When you're making a declaration, you have to put individual milestones aside. It's a team-first mentality every time. If a batsman is heading towards a milestone—a century or a century on debut—you might send out a message: 'We're going to declare at four o'clock. That's your opportunity to make the hundred or not.' If they're really close to the landmark, the captain might delay his call for a few more minutes. Otherwise, declare and that's the way it is. It's a team game, first and foremost.

Follow-ons are interesting in this context, especially in the modern game. Once upon a time there was a rest day in Test matches, which was a big factor because the bowlers could put their feet up for a day. Nowadays there's no rest day, but in the past it was tempting to have a second crack at a team, given your bowlers would get a day's rest. I think India gave captains around the world plenty to think about when they won a Test match against Steve Waugh's Australian team at Kolkata in 2001 after following on.

That was an absolutely amazing game. Australia made 445 then bowled India out for 171, leaving Waugh to make a decision. With a lead of 274 he chose to enforce the follow-on, which can only be applied by a captain if his team is 200 runs ahead on the first innings. Then V.V.S. Laxman and Rahul Dravid came together at 4–232, still 42 in arrears, and batted for an entire day! Australia's bowlers ended up churning through more than 200 overs in a row without any break, Laxman and Dravid put on 376 runs for the fifth wicket, India set Australia 384 to win and then bowled Waugh's team out for 212 on the final day.

It was a perfect storm that worked against an Australian team that had dominated the first part of the match, but it did make captains think about the follow-on a little more afterwards, I've no doubt. It brought back memories, because of only three Test matches that have actually been won by teams that followed on, I played in one—the famous 1981 Leeds Test when Ian Botham and Bob Willis dug England out of a hole. The other match was in the 19th century. Believe me, it's not a good feeling to be on the receiving end! That explains why captains tend to wave off the follow-on and have a second bat nowadays, to rest up their bowlers for a second assault on the opposition.

DARREN LEHMANN AS coach of Australia from 2013 brought back some old-fashioned values: play hard, enjoy the fruits of your labours, encourage the boys to stay in the rooms. If the boys don't want to have an alcoholic drink—and there are plenty of those guys today—they should have water or something soft. Those edicts have worked in our cricket for 100 years.

Lehmann tried to lighten the mood, too: 'We're working hard, let's have some fun. Let's play cricket like Australians play cricket.' I think it eased a lot of tension around the place. Guys had reached the point where they weren't enjoying playing for Australia, which the results showed, with the 4–0 defeat in India in 2013. Despite Cricket Australia sacking Mickey Arthur as coach after the Indian disaster and hiring Lehmann, we still had a 3–0 defeat in the 2013 Ashes series in England.

Before that, 'Boof' Lehmann had been a breath of fresh air as coach of Queensland, and the players still talk about how enjoyable their cricket was during that period, when they won both the Sheffield Shield and the Ryobi Cup one-day competition. Lehmann's mantra when he took over from Mickey Arthur was the same: work hard, play hard. You still get your feedback from your computer analysts and maintain your fitness levels, but that's not the be-all and end-all. You're a bowler, so you bowl. You're a batsman, so you bat.

There's none of that structured rotation of players now, or limits on how many balls you might bowl, unless you're recovering from an injury. They have a set program, but if you're a bowler, you bowl in the nets, keep up your skills, teach your body what it's about. I understand that sports science has taken us to new levels with the game, but I think we need to step back a bit in order to go forward.

IMPORTANTLY, MICHAEL CLARKE and Darren Lehmann are a good fit as captain and coach, I guess in a similar way to Bob Simpson and me. They fit together as a team, even though they're quite different people. Michael's the metrosexual and Boof is a knockabout bloke, but it's working—it's a good marriage. They may be opposites to some extent, but they respect each other. Michael can concentrate on what he does best—batting and getting his 20 wickets. Darren creates the atmosphere and the mood. He sets the work ethic.

Mitchell Johnson is a good example of how the Clarke–Lehmann partnership has worked for Australia. They've told Mitchell to bowl fast, in short spells. Before that, Mitchell was getting advice from a lot of different people—coaches trying to get him to swing the ball, saying, 'Your arm's too low, it needs to be higher' or 'You need to keep it to two runs an over.' It wasn't Mitchell's style; it didn't work at all for him to be bowling like that. He was a special bowler before that, and he always had the ability to bowl quickly, with more than 200 wickets to show for it. The results in the home Ashes series of 2013–14—where he took 37 wickets at 13.97 to help win the series for Australia—speak for themselves. It was a remarkable turnaround and it was due to clever handling of a very talented player.

Not many people in the history of the game have been able to bowl at 150 km/h and put it on a sixpence all the time. The effort it takes to bowl that fast leaves you with that spray factor, and that's part of the beauty of it, because it can also make it very difficult for the batsman, a little unpredictable. It was a nightmare to bat against Jeff Thomson in my time, for instance, because he was that kind of bowler, quick but unpredictable. Mitchell had a horror time in England in 2009. He was getting clattered around, but he also wasn't bowling anywhere near that 150 km/h mark, and he was totally confused about what Mitchell Johnson is best at: running in, doing what comes naturally and getting the ball to the other end at good pace. If it swings, then great, if it doesn't, then who cares, because it's still quick.

Lehmann and Clarke gave him carte blanche: 'Don't worry about if it goes down leg side or off side, your role is as the enforcer. We want you to bowl a lot of bouncers, get stuck into them. You'll bowl about four overs in a spell.' Now, Mitchell knows that four overs won't kill him, so he goes flat out. He can bowl 16 or 18 overs at top pace through a day because he knows he won't be asked to bowl 25 overs in a day. If he were, he might ease back a fraction.

There comes a point when you say, 'What's best for Mitchell?' He's very athletic and he can bowl fast, although he doesn't necessarily swing it, because of his slinging action. When he does swing it, he's a nightmare to face. So just let him bowl, and if it's not working, get him off. They used him really well against England and he had a catastrophic effect. When he was on, the game moved at a rapid rate.

Mitchell Johnson's extreme pace is a great asset, albeit one you can't buy off the shelf, more's the pity. Johnson has more than 250 Test wickets, which is a great record, yet it's not so long ago that he was maligned. How ironic! Mitchell was confused about all the advice, and he's the type of guy who needs to keep it simple and enjoy his cricket. When you wake up in the morning and you have to drag yourself out of bed to go and play or practise, how can you play your best? That's why I like the Lehmann style.

To a coach like Darren Lehmann, it's about creating the right environment. It needs to be fun. You jump out of bed as a player, and you have a productive day. In Australia, we've always enjoyed the fruits of winning, and if we won, we celebrated, let the pressure valve out a little. Otherwise, why are you playing?

My era was wonderful, but I'd make two concessions to the modern game: we should have drunk less and trained harder, to get fitter and stronger. I wasn't too bad, I was match-fit, but a bit of weight training would have made a difference with fatigue and decision-making late in the day. Golfers do it now and it helps over four rounds. If I had my time again, I'd up the ante with my preparation and do more skills work—more batting, bowling and fielding.

I tried to reduce the players' alcohol consumption for a while when I was captain of Queensland. In those days, we went on a southern swing where we'd play Tasmania, Victoria and maybe South Australia, and invariably we'd play poorly. It was a major issue for Queensland that we played well at the Gabba but badly away from home, and we were looking for reasons why. It was costing us dearly; we might finish third in the Sheffield Shield but we'd dominated at home. I said, 'Look, boys, we're drinking too much. Simple as that.' I know that John Scholes, when he was coach of Victoria, had the same thinking— players tended to drink too much when they were on the road.

When we were playing for Queensland at the Gabba, we might have a couple of beers in the rooms and then go home. But on the road we might have half a dozen beers a night, maybe more, every night for three weeks, and by the time we got to the last game, we were in Victoria, and we performed like shot ducks. We played rubbish cricket.

I think we drank too much back then, but to be fair, it was just part of the culture. It didn't harm anyone too much in terms of results, because *everyone* was doing it, and even the best teams won at home but struggled on the road. More recently, players have become more efficient with their eating and drinking habits, and in the Shield now they seem to be winning more often away from home. Queensland could never win in Perth; they do now. New South Wales were the same. Other states now beat Queensland at the Gabba; that *never* used to happen. Teams have looked for ways to improve and that was one way, to cut down or stop drinking. It has a cumulative effect over four days if you treat being on the road like party mode.

I don't feel like I was an alcoholic, but when I was young we'd have three–four beers minimum in the rooms, then go out for a meal and have another couple, and then we might go to a pub afterwards to wash it down. It all adds up and it was far too much.

SLEDGING IS PART of the game. The first time I can recall copping it myself was from a guy called Brian Riley, a bit of a legend in Sydney grade cricket and also baseball. He was probably in his early twenties and I was about 16, walking out to bat for Mosman. He must have been at cover and as I went past I heard, 'Jesus Christ, what have we got here? Sending a boy on a man's mission!' I was petrified. I'd come out of the lower grades and I'd never been picked at like that. It stuck with me.

Sledging itself is a fairly modern phenomenon. There's always been chat, but these days people talk about chat and sledging as if they're the same thing, as if every time someone says something on a cricket field they're sledging, which isn't the case at all. Is something like, 'We've got to stick it up this bloke. Get another slip in!' sledging? To me, it's gamesmanship—chirping but not sledging. Sledging is abuse. 'I'm going to knock your fucking head off, mate!' That's sledging.

My understanding of the origin of the term 'sledging' goes back to John Benaud, the former New South Wales and Australian batsman who became a national selector. It was a reference to Len Pascoe, the fast bowler from the eighties, who was as mad as a cut snake with a cricket ball in his hand, and would rant and rave and sledge even if he was the nicest bloke in the world off the field. John Benaud said, 'Lennie, as usual you're as subtle as a sledgehammer.' I think that's where it came from.

Then there's the 'send-off', when a batsman cops a pasting after he's been dismissed and he's on his way to the pavilion. My first send-off was from a guy called Steve Taylor, who played for North Sydney, an old Mosman boy. I hit him for four fours in a row in a grade game, then I went for a slash and chopped it back onto my stumps. He gave me a massive send-off.

I witnessed some swearing in Sydney grade cricket. A lot of the cricketers played baseball and there's a lot of chirping in baseball, and that found its way into cricket. But a bit of chirp doesn't bother me, although I don't like kids at under-12 level having a crack at another player in an abusive way, so we have to be careful. It's hard to tell a kid to stop when he just comes back with, 'So-and-so does it when I watch it on TV.' It's a fine line.

The key to keeping it in hand is good umpiring. We had strong umpires who would jump on it pretty quickly—like Dickie Bird and David Shepherd and Peter Willey, for instance—and those guys could defuse any issues quite easily. But players can lose the plot under pressure, of course, and there are blokes who get up your nose. The Pakistan batsman Javed Miandad used to play us on a break, and Sri Lanka's ex-captain Arjuna Ranatunga was another guy who had an uncanny knack of getting our hackles up. But there's always a line to be drawn: we can't have racist abuse, we can't have outright abuse.

Australians are swearers generally, and we'll drop the magic word without thinking twice; the F-word will come out in the workplace and it's not necessarily being abusive. It's in our manner to be a bit derogatory to other people, even to friends and colleagues, in that sarcastic way: 'You're a goose, mate.' They're not fighting words, it's just our vernacular. But West Indians, and Indians in particular, don't much like cursing or swearing, so if we say, 'Get back and fucking bat now,' they can take it personally. The West Indians used to say, 'Don't curse me, man!'

So there are cultural differences at play. In Australia you might call someone a 'lucky bastard' and it's almost a term of endearment. Sometimes you might say loudly to a bowler, 'This guy's got no fucking idea.' It's only banter in my mind, and you're trying to get inside a bloke's head, but there's absolutely no harm intended. You'll get together with that batsman later and have a beer and say, 'Gee, I thought we had you there.' It's part of the battle. In Australia we play hard cricket, which comes from the Sheffield Shield, which has always been a hard competition, yet generally the guys get on really well. They'll catch up with each other after a day's play, and there are no grudges. That doesn't always work with overseas teams, though.

The Indian Premier League (IPL) has broken down a few barriers, because the Indians and some players from other countries can see now that we're just mucking around when we talk like that on the field. When the batsman Kepler Wessels came to Australia from South Africa he had a lot of trouble with our vernacular and the way we spoke and swore at each other. He couldn't quite get it, the rhyming slang and that kind of stuff, and *he's* South African. Imagine how it sounds to the Indians and West Indians, who are just not the slightest bit accustomed to that kind of behaviour.

We do play an 'in your face' type of game so we can't moan if it comes back at us. The camera comes in close and everyone's chirping, and I suppose the opposition looks at Australian sides and doesn't want to take a backward step: 'We know that the Aussies are going to come at us. They'll try to intimidate us with pace bowling and verbals, so we'll give as good as we get. We've been copping it for years, that's it.' I reckon that's the way they'd look at it.

It's a harsh word, 'cheating'. Does cheating mean you know you've caught a ball on the bounce? That's cheating if you *know* you're in the wrong. But it's interesting, because I wasn't a walker when I batted. So if you nick the ball, and you know you nicked it but you stand and wait for the umpire's decision, what's the difference?

With catches, you'll cop heaps from the opposition if you've caught the ball on the bounce. But if a guy nicks and doesn't walk, players will be aggrieved but not for long. He might get sledged but the comeback would be: 'You've never nicked one and not walked?'

Adam Gilchrist made a personal decision to walk when he was out. He decided to play the game in a certain way, and that's fine, but it's not necessarily the Australian way. Our way is to let the umpire make the decision, and if he says you're out, you get off the ground.

In England, when I first played county cricket for Essex in 1986, I was told, 'Mate, the county system will get you if you don't walk. Just be aware.' What invariably happened was that if you nicked one and didn't walk, it got around the umpiring fraternity, and the next five times you batted they'd give you out if the ball hit your pad. It was like: 'Have you got the message yet?' So I started walking for the first time in my life. For the two years I played county cricket at Essex, I walked because that was the culture. I thought, 'This is the way they're playing it. I don't want to get fired the next time.' It's not such a bad system. The umpires make decisions on lbw and tight run-outs, and then if you nicked it, you go.

But the trouble with walking is that the game has become more and more professional. It's easy to operate like that when you're an amateur and you have a day job, but if you're thinking, 'If I make runs today I'm a chance for the Test team, and if I make the Test team I go from a $150,000 contract to a $500,000 contract,' that's different. When there's money in the equation, it does change the way guys behave. Hats off to Adam Gilchrist, who once walked in a World Cup semi-final in South Africa when he was given not out to a caught-behind appeal off Aravinda de Silva of Sri Lanka. That one raised a few eyebrows, because of the gravity of the match and the moment. I thought, 'Bloody hell, this is a semi-final!' But he stayed true to his philosophy; he turned and walked, and Australia won anyway, on their way to a triumph in the final.

Sometimes with bat-pad decisions you're not 100 per cent sure as a batsman. There are times when you know you haven't hit the ball and you're given out, and over a career it probably evens out. That's how I justify to myself *not* walking.

I FELT VERY sorry for Greg Dyer, who was caught up in an incident during a Test against New Zealand at the Melbourne Cricket Ground (MCG) in the summer of 1987–88. Greg was a stand-up guy, but he ended up getting vilified. Andrew Jones of New Zealand feathered a ball down the leg side from Craig McDermott's bowling, Greg dived, got gloves to the ball and then rolled. Jones was given out, caught behind, and I can honestly say that from second slip, I thought he caught it. I'm absolutely sure that if he knew he'd dropped that catch, he'd have said, 'No, no, that's not out,' and we'd have recalled Jones. But Greg wasn't sure, so at the time we moved on. Then the replays showed that the ball had touched the ground and, as happens in cases like this, the mud started to fly. These days, you'd have the opportunity to refer it. Back then, it just blew up on us. 'There's absolutely no doubt that ball has hit the ground and wicket-keeper Dyer has claimed a catch that doesn't look to me like it was one,' said Tony Greig on Channel Nine's coverage.

Dyer was distraught once he found out it hadn't carried. He is a straight bloke, and it would never enter his mind to do something like that. Some guys would claim anything, but Greg's not that kind of guy. It was a mistake and he felt bad about it. It affected his cricket; he only played two more Test matches, and he was finished as a Test player by February 1988. From that point on, we were searching for the keeper-batsman, and Tim Zoehrer from Western Australia was still around, too, but Ian Healy ended up coming into the team as keeper-batsman in 1988.

So we play hard but I'd like to think we wouldn't resort to blatant cheating. If we make a mistake, it's a genuine mistake, and we'd tend to get it referred rather than claim it. Rod Marsh called back the English batsman Derek Randall in the Centenary Test in 1977 when 'Bacchus' knew a low catch had bounced but the umpire had given it out.

The Australian way

In the past, the batsmen or the umpires used to ask the fieldsman if he'd taken a low catch, and they'd accept his word. When Ricky Ponting was captain of Australia, he tried to have that system instituted again, but some other teams wouldn't have it, and when it was in place, it caused issues as well. A lot of the trust has gone nowadays.

With those low catches, the referrals invariably go in the batsman's favour, even though sometimes the fieldsman will *know* he's caught it as clean as a whistle. The ball *looks* like it hits the ground, and you can't see fingers under it. Sometimes you can feel the thump of the ball squeezing your fingers rather than bouncing up off the turf, although I can't say you're always 100 per cent sure with those low ones.

I HAD THE pleasure of playing with Shane Warne for a couple of years, from his debut in 1991 through to the South African tour of 1994, and he was a freak of a player. I liked him straight away. He's disarming, good company and interesting; he acts the same way around all manner of people, and they're drawn to him. Of course he's led with his chin and made a few mistakes in his life, but he's openly admitted his faults and moved on. I know he's been a good father to his kids, giving them a lot of time and making sure they have stability in their lives.

I knew he had something special when we first saw him, when he was picked to play the Test match against India at Sydney in 1992, and Ravi Shastri and a young Sachin Tendulkar hit him around the park, Shastri on his way to making a double century. Jim Higgs was a selector at the time, and he'd said, 'I've got this bloke in Melbourne, he's a bit raw, but there's something about him.' That something was a massive leg-spinner that fizzed in the air and swerved. Credit to the selectors for trying him after just a handful of Sheffield Shield matches for Victoria.

But he was no overnight sensation. 'Warnie' took 1–150 in that match, even though he bowled well at times, and some of the reviews were less than encouraging. There's the famous line from Kerry O'Keeffe, himself a leggie from the past: 'Too fat, can't bowl' or something like that! Bill O'Reilly was impressed, and Rodney Hogg even more so. Having seen him just the once, 'Hoggy' wrote in his column for *The Truth* newspaper that the boy would take 500 Test wickets. Needless to say, it was a big call, and as Warne's captain, I was immediately asked about that. I said, 'Look, there's something there, but 500 Test wickets? I don't know.' History shows that he went a little further; he finished with 708 Test wickets, another 293 in one-day internationals, and is acclaimed as probably the best spin bowler in the history of the game.

What we learnt quite quickly was that Warne was a sponge for information. We took him to Sri Lanka on tour in 1992, and after taking 0–107 in the first innings of the First Test, he took three late wickets in the second without conceding a run, helping us win in Colombo. He learnt from the early troubles. He'd turned up in Sydney a bit overweight, and he looked like he'd been spending way too much time at St Kilda Beach. Ian McDonald, our manager, had sprung him with a pie and a beer at the Boxing Day Test and possibly a cigarette as well, for the trifecta. But by the time we went to Sri Lanka he was fitter, he'd done some technical work with Terry Jenner, the former Test leg-spinner who would become his mentor, and he was a different beast.

Warnie started out with mainly a big leg-spinner, then a back-spinner and a wrong 'un and the famous flipper. Later in his career he bowled a slider that didn't do much but looked like a leg-spinner, and he was always talking up his variety. There was an element of bluff to this, I've no doubt—nobody ever did mind games better than him. He was always telling the press he had a new ball to start the new season, and it would draw a headline about his 'mystery ball'. This was part of the fabric and the mystique of Warne, who was wonderful for the game.

Warne used his brain and worked out ways to dismiss batsmen, starting out with the big leg-spinner and the nicks to slip and to the keeper, then later on with the skidding ball sliding straight on for the lbw or the bowled. Around 1992–94 he was sensational with the flipper— the ball that's flicked out between the fingers and comes out much quicker then goes on straight—starting out by bowling Richie Richardson with that ball at the MCG in the Melbourne Test against the West Indies in 1992–93. It became an amazing weapon for him, but after he popped his shoulder it was never quite the same. He still accumulated wickets in other ways, though. I must admit as captain that we tended to overuse him because he was so good. It was easy for the skipper to look around and say, 'I'll just keep Warnie bowling.' He was a captain's dream.

ON THE 1993 Ashes tour, we held Warne back in the lead-up to the Test matches, with some success. England hadn't seen him, of course, although his reputation had travelled, because he'd bowled out the West Indies that day at the MCG for an Australian win and taken the world by storm. We knew full well he was special, and we weren't about to give the English players a heads-up on the sorcerer until they confronted him in a Test match.

We left him out of the one-dayers at the start of the tour, and even though he played in a tour game at Worcester before the First Test at Old Trafford, we pulled him out of the attack and told him not to show too much. Warnie was very frustrated with me, because he was bowling at Graeme Hick, who knocked him around a bit, and we knew Hick would be playing for England in the Tests. I said, 'Warnie, play dumb here. Just roll them out. Don't show him anything because he'll be in the England side.'

Hick made 187, Warnie took 1–122 and he was ropeable. But there were more important battles to come.

The big day arrived at Old Trafford in Manchester, the first Test match. We held the Ashes from our win at home in 1990–91, but England knocked us over for 289 on a tacky pitch, and had reached 1–80 when I threw the ball to Warnie. We knew the pitch was offering some spin, because their off-spinner Peter Such had taken six of our wickets, so it was nicely set up for the great man playing his first Test against the old enemy. So began the legend.

You could always tell whether Warnie was bowling at his best by the amount of swerve he imparted to the ball, from off to leg, purely because of the rotations on the ball. This first delivery went a long way, dipping in and outside the leg stump of Mike Gatting, who was on strike. Actually, 'Gatt' didn't do too much wrong in the way he handled it, trying to let it hit his body since it was pitching way outside leg stump and could never have been given out lbw. But that ball pitched and spun right past him and into the off stump and he walked off in total shock. The look on his face was priceless.

Aside from Warnie, and Ian Healy behind the stumps, I'm not sure any of us knew exactly how good that single delivery, the so-called 'Ball of the Century', had been. From where I was fielding at short cover, all I saw was the ball hitting the castle. Even Richie Benaud's commentary was a bit incredulous. It wasn't until we all saw the replay during a break in play that we realised exactly how good that ball was.

Twenty years on, Mike Gatting still cops it from Australians about that moment, and I myself never miss a chance to remind him of his other malfunction, the reverse sweep to be dismissed in the 1987 World Cup at Kolkata from my bowling. He often says, 'Bloody hell, you Australians. I played two bad shots in my life and I never hear the end of it!' Warnie took 34 wickets in the series, we won the Ashes easily, and the world of cricket had a new superstar.

I WAS FORTUNATE in that the critics never savaged me too often. Occasionally there'd be a media-driven story, and Neil Harvey might jump out and deliver a quote. As a selector, 'Harv' had originally picked me for the team, and I had no problem with him, although he'd been known to say about me, 'It's time for him to go.' I suppose there were periods when I deserved it, but I didn't have any lingering issues with him.

You have to cop it as a player, and when I was captain the criticism was probably justified, especially early on. I was equally self-critical, so I wasn't about to get upset with the media, with whom I had a good relationship. I tried to shoot as straight as I could, and I think the media gathered I was doing my best. I also never had the kind of really long slump as a player that would have left me vulnerable. The way I played wasn't foolproof, but because I wasn't an extravagant player, I played the margins better than most.

Ian Chappell criticised me, but it was never personal. He often wrote that my captaincy was too conservative, and that I allowed Bob Simpson too much power as coach. I've spent time with 'Chappelli' over the years, often in a bar. We generally have strong discussions, but he *likes* arguing. He's an argumentative person, not always right but never wrong! He challenges me but I get a lot out of those conversations. It's good-natured banter.

I think he wanted me to take hold of the job as captain, and no doubt he was right. My captaincy career fell into two halves: the 'Why am I doing this job?' period, when my decisions were affected, and the results didn't come; and then the period when I got it and was a little more proactive and took some more risks. The early criticism I've got no problem with. I'm critical myself of the way I handled the taking of the job as captain.

Players react differently to the critics. In a team of 11 there will always be a percentage who are touchy-feely guys who don't like criticism, who prefer to have their tyres pumped up rather than let down. There are guys who couldn't care less, and others still who actually enjoy it and are motivated by it. Teams need that diversity in order to be a collective force. It sounds funny, but you can't have all type-A personalities because the strong personalities will end up clashing. The collective is stronger when you have a mix of personalities and people know they can be themselves.

AUSTRALIA HAS SOME red-hot talent in the ranks at the moment, and especially in the fast-bowling department. Some of these lads could be extra special if they can get their bodies to cooperate and stay on the park. They've had a taste, shown they're capable of being top-shelf players and, in a couple of cases, broken down with injuries. But they'll be back, I'm sure.

Take Mitchell Starc, the left-armer who at 196 centimetres tall is just so athletic. Not only can he bowl, but his batting is so good that he can virtually become an all-rounder. He has a great package to offer, but he needs some luck with his injuries. It's up to Darren Lehmann and the coaching staff to prise the best from him when he has that moment of clarity good players tend to have.

James Pattinson, the Victorian quick, is another player I really like. He has that fast bowler's mongrel attitude, which is important. He's quick, he swings the ball, he's aggressive by nature, he can bat a bit and field, and he has a good head on his shoulders. Of course his back has let him down a couple of times, but this is the point about fast bowlers. We can't mollycoddle them. Accept that they'll break down occasionally and hope it's not career-threatening. And accept that some players—Bruce Reid was an example from my time—won't necessarily be great for 15 years. They might only extract six or seven years, and so be it.

Patrick Cummins is another example of an unfulfilled talent, having broken down with a back injury soon after he made his sensational Test debut at the Wanderers in Johannesburg, South Africa, in 2011, taking seven wickets and getting some valuable runs in the chase for victory. He has that vital ingredient of compelling 150 km/h pace, and he's made a first-grade century with the bat. Yes, he's had stress fractures, but if he's fit and available, I'd play him and I'd have him bowl quite a lot at 75–80 per cent intensity in the nets, to turn the engine over. Cummins is an amazing talent, and if we can put these bowlers all on the park at once, we'll have a hell of a team.

BEFORE THE ERA of coaches, the senior players did a lot of the mentoring in Australian cricket. As a young guy, you did best to shut up and listen. But when I first played in 1978–79, it was the time of the great World Series Cricket (WSC) split; we were thrown into the swimming pool of Test cricket and whether we sank or swam was up to us. The team vibe was a little like every man for himself, and blokes were looking over their shoulders wondering who would get the knife next. It wasn't the best cricket environment.

When the WSC players came back in 1980, I probably felt more welcome than the first time I played. I just sat in the rooms until they all went. I hardly said boo, spoke when spoken to, and if they were there at ten o'clock at night, so was I. It was brilliant. I had a good relationship with Greg Chappell, who was the captain. Greg had an aloofness about him; it's the way he is, but cricket was also a fairly easy game for him—he was a great fielder, good bowler, great batsman. But he was helpful to me, once I asked him, 'Can you have a look at me in the nets?' We didn't have a coach in those days, just a manager who travelled with the team to handle the administration. The senior players coached the team, setting the tone for how we played, how we behaved, everything, and the captain ran the show. I never had a problem with Greg, and I took it upon myself to ask him questions.

THE BAGGY GREEN cap is sacred but there's been a subtle change in the way it's handled. When I first started playing, we used to swap them with opponents and the board would provide another. I'd have had 15 in my time, whereas in the modern era they need to sign a statutory declaration to have it replaced. I gave one to Johnny Raper, the great St George rugby league player who was my idol growing up, and I gave one to Elton John. This was before Steve Waugh, as captain in the nineties, went about making it a big deal, with the formal presentation of the cap and the allocation of a number to define you as an Australian Test cricketer, which I applaud.

I swapped my cap and jumper with Javed Miandad after the series against Pakistan at home in 1978–79, which in hindsight is one of the most acrimonious series played. In Melbourne, where I scored my first Test hundred, Miandad had run out Rodney Hogg while he was doing some gardening down the pitch. Hoggy couldn't believe it and smashed down the stumps. Then in Perth, Asif Iqbal made a great century, batting with the tail, and we couldn't get him out. We wanted to get their No. 11, Sikander Bakht, on strike as much as possible, but he was backing up way too far so that they could take the quick single and keep Iqbal on strike.

At drinks, we discussed it, and we decided to warn Sikander that we'd 'Mankad' him—run him out at the non-striker's end—if he kept backing up too early. Unfortunately, Alan Hurst, our quick bowler, immediately smashed the stumps down and ran Sikander out without offering the customary warning. It was only the fourth time it had happened in the history of Test cricket, and we were in shock. We probably should have called him back and said, 'That's your warning,' but we didn't.

The Pakistanis were furious, and when we batted on the same day, Andrew Hilditch was given out 'handled the ball'. A throw came in from the outfield with Sarfraz Nawaz bowling, and 'Sarf' dropped the ball, letting it roll towards Hilditch, who picked it up and handed it to the bowler. Sarfraz immediately appealed, and Hilditch was given out. Now I know a batsman isn't allowed to handle the ball, but the ball was dead in that instance. He wasn't even the striker at the time. He wasn't impeding play or trying to pinch a run, but the emotions were at boiling point. Asif Iqbal later said he couldn't believe Pakistan had stooped so low as to appeal in that instance. But we were also guilty.

It was an acrimonious introduction to Test cricket but I did get on well with Javed Miandad. He's in the top half-dozen I played against, a great bloke and a fighter. He was a feisty competitor, and he certainly knew how to push our buttons.

THE SHEFFIELD SHIELD is a big part of our strength as a cricketing nation. We're lucky there are so few states, because it means our talent is corralled into six teams, which is ideal. I love the fact that we play ten games, and that it's highly competitive. I'd hate to see Cricket Australia cut those matches back. I know it's difficult to fit all the different strands into the program, but I'd let it stand alone, and if Test players can only play a couple of games, so be it.

The Australian way

The Shield costs a lot to run, but a good company would consider that to be research and development. There's a strong return on that investment, and the players love it. I believe it's worth the money because you develop your best players through Shield rather than the Ryobi Cup or the Big Bash. It's hard cricket that produces players who are ready for international cricket, because it simulates top-level cricket between nations. I actually played Shield matches that were as tough as Test matches, and that's why I like the concept of the five-day Sheffield Shield final. A lot of people don't like it, because it favours the home team, which only needs a draw to collect the title. It doesn't bother me that the home team has to be beaten by the visiting team. It's happened before—not often, but it *is* possible.

The top side has earned the right to host the final, and the other team has five days to win the game. If they can't do it, tough luck. I think it's a game worth keeping on the calendar, the closest thing to a Test match some of those guys will ever play. If they never play a Test match, then at least they'll have played at that level of cricket.

If you're playing for Australia, though, I'd like to think you have a national team ethic and put state rivalries aside. Sure, if you play against each other in a Sheffield Shield match or a one-dayer or Twenty20 match, then you'll try to bash each other, and that's fine. But it's not like being in England, where the people of the north speak differently from the people of the south, or even the west. In England, there's a tribal mentality, and to see that in action you need only look at their soccer and the passions it incites.

In Australia we tend to speak the same way, and we don't have the historical differences, like the red rose and white rose, Lancashire versus Yorkshire, or any big religious differences, or the obvious racial divide of South Africa, for instance. Even the West Indies as a cricket entity have differences, with jealousies between the various islands, whose people don't always get on. We're lucky that our system is an Australia-first system: the pinnacle is the Australian cricket team and everything is geared towards that.

AUSTRALIAN CRICKET TEAMS have always given fielding a high priority, and it's helped us on the international stage. In my time, it was a massive focus for every training session, and I've no doubt it's the same today. When I played, there'd be some moaning at the end of a tough net session when we were told to do some fielding, but we'd do it. There's no doubt it helps. Probably the oldest saying in cricket is 'Catches win matches', and it's very true.

We had an advantage with our fielding over the years, and I think we generally take our catches and create run-out chances a little better than most sides. But the truth is that other nations are getting better, getting smarter, catching up. The best Australian sides all had good slip fieldsmen and good all-round fieldsmen. We had a Ricky Ponting, or more recently a David Warner, who could pull off a miraculous stop and then run someone out with a direct hit. It makes a big difference; it's a momentum shifter when you create something from nothing. It might be the opposition's best player, and that changes the mood around a cricket team.

In the old days, the Indians would never dive in the field, because at home they'd take off skin on their rough grounds, but they don't have that excuse now their grounds have improved immensely. The West Indians, on the other hand, were an athletic team and a fine fielding team, but they didn't dive much either, because the grounds in the Caribbean were too hard. Perhaps they were so good they didn't need to dive!

The best fieldsman I've seen? Roger Harper of the West Indies would be in the final. He was invariably their 12th man in my playing days, even if he was never going to play. They'd roll him out when someone was indisposed or injured, and he was magnificent. Viv Richards was right up there, and they say that Clive Lloyd was the 'Supercat' in his day. When I played against Clive, he was older and he'd stand in the slips, where he was very good. Jonty Rhodes of South Africa was excellent, and Ricky Ponting was superb, just brilliant with his direct hits on the stumps. Andrew Symonds had an incredibly strong arm, and Mark Waugh was as good as it gets as an all-round fieldsman. Of the English players, David Gower was graceful and outstanding, Derek Randall used to throw himself around, and Ian Botham was a fabulous slipper who could also field well at bat-pad.

I rate Ponting and Mark Waugh highly because they could catch a high ball on the fence, field in slips or do it in the covers. Michael Clarke's a wonderful fielder; he has beautiful hands and he can throw blokes out when fielding in close. Most of the top cricketers were also good fielders. Like Greg Chappell. I can't remember him dropping an outfield catch, and he had soft hands in the slip cordon, too. A lot of the best have been Australians, which is no fluke. We've recognised for a long time that fielding is super-important.

THE BEST CATCHES aren't necessarily the most spectacular. In the modern era with Twenty20 cricket, we see some incredible athletic acts in the field—guys taking catches on the boundary rope, tossing the ball back into the playing arena to complete the dismissal, and hurling themselves around the field. Throughout history there have always been catches where players threw themselves and the ball stuck, like John Dyson's famous catch at the SCG against the West Indies in 1982, flinging himself to dismiss Sylvester Clarke like a soccer goalkeeper. There's no fluke in that;

'Dyso' did play some soccer before he made the Australian cricket team, and he *was* a goalkeeper!

Steve Waugh took a great outfield catch from Roger Harper in a one-day international against the West Indies at the MCG one night in 1988–89, running behind the sight screen after completing the catch. And the all-rounder Dan Christian took an amazing catch playing a Twenty20 international for Australia against Pakistan in Dubai fairly recently, running back with the flight and launching himself to take it. Funnily enough, one great catch I remember was taken by Paul 'Fatty' Vautin, the Queensland rugby league legend, in my testimonial match at the Gabba in 1993! Timmy Horan, the Wallaby, was the batsman, and he skied a ball from Allan Langer's bowling toward square leg, sending Fatty hurtling after it at odds of roughly a million to one of actually catching it. But he ran 35 metres, put out his right hand and it stuck, then he just kept running for the celebration. When he came back to the huddle he just said, 'What's the big deal? That's what you're supposed to do, isn't it?'

The best catch I took was at slip to dismiss New Zealander John Reid at the Gabba in 1985–86, a full-length dive taken in my left hand. But really, I think the best catches are reflex takes, close to the bat or at slip from a spinner, for instance. The guys who field at bat-pad have to deal with the fear factor as well as the skill question, and David Boon took some brilliant snares in there during my time. I've seen Mark Taylor and Mark Waugh take some incredible catches at slip from batsmen rocking back and cutting, in particular one from Shane Warne's bowling to Inzamam-ul-Haq at Bellerive Oval in 1999, which 'Junior' caught in his right hand, clean as you like. The ball seems to fly quicker from the flashing blade, and Inzamam made a full swing at the shot. These are the catches that cricketers rate highest, even if they don't necessarily make the highlight reel.

HISTORY WILL SHOW our side of the late nineties in a very good light, but I still maintain that I can't imagine any cricket team ever getting the better of the West Indies team of the mid-seventies to early nineties over a five-Test series. They didn't lose a full series for 15 years. I know that Australia's winning rate was higher, because the West Indies played a few more draws. The West Indies played with a wear-down factor and a group of fast bowlers so good they didn't have a weak link. I couldn't say Australia's team from about 1999 onward was better, but it would be a series to salivate over!

I reckon four of that Australian side would probably be in our best-ever team, while with the West Indies you could probably argue that many more would be in their best ever. Are Desmond Haynes, Gordon Greenidge and Viv Richards better than Frank Worrell, Everton Weekes, Clyde Walcott and Learie Constantine? Wes Hall might get a guernsey in their best bowling attack, but how do you fit in Andy Roberts, Malcolm Marshall, Joel Garner, Michael Holding and Curtly Ambrose? Garry Sobers would also get a spot! Australia would challenge them, and you could say the same for South Africa in the seventies and England in the early eighties.

Our team should have beaten the West Indies at home in the summer of 1992–93. We'd prepared ourselves to dethrone the men from the Caribbean, who hadn't lost a Test series since their tour of New Zealand in 1980. Viv Richards and Gordon Greenidge had retired, Craig McDermott was up with the West Indian pair of Curtly Ambrose and Courtney Walsh among the best quick bowlers in the world, and we'd discovered a leg-spinner named Shane Warne. But we couldn't finish them off.

We were 1–0 up going to Adelaide for the Fourth Test, and a win would have closed out the series. Merv Hughes (5–64) was heroic in the first innings, then in their second innings Tim May took 5–9 with his off-spinners, leaving us 186 to win, a manageable ask. But we stumbled, at one point reaching 7–74 before May and Craig McDermott dug in. It was one of Test cricket's most famous finishes, and it teased us all the way to the inglorious end.

Needing two runs for the match win and the series, McDermott whipped a ball off his legs and Desmond Haynes at bat-pad somehow stopped it with an outstretched hand. Two balls later, Walsh bounced McDermott and umpire

Darrell Hair gave him out caught behind, caught off the glove and helmet, a contentious decision to this day. In the viewing room, the 'worry ball' I'd been tossing around went flying. Ambrose had taken six wickets and the series was tied. A week later, on their favourite Perth deck, the West Indians smashed us and won the series 2–1. I never played in a winning series against them, the closest being a 1–1 draw in 1981–82. They were too good.

AUSTRALIA HAS CHOPPED and changed and never quite settled on whether the captain and coach should be selectors. On tour, of course, it always tended to be different, because in my day there were no selectors on an overseas trip, and so the skipper and coach needed to be selectors even though they hadn't been involved in picking the original team.

At one point Bob Simpson as coach became a selector, but this privilege was later removed from 'Simmo', the feeling being that players who were struggling for form or confidence might have trouble approaching the coach if they knew he was a selector. We might have been ahead of our time with that decision, and it's worth remembering that we didn't have anywhere near the number of support staff in those days. It made a certain amount of sense to have the coach as a selector then, as it does now. But the captain was never a selector in my time, and in fact in my early years as skipper I wasn't even consulted on selection. That changed in the latter part of my tenure, and rightly so.

After the Australian team lost the Ashes in 2009, Cricket Australia commissioned the Argus review into team performance at the elite level, and the issue of captain and coach as selectors came up again. I sat on the commission with Don Argus, Steve Waugh, Mark Taylor and Malcolm Speed—the former Cricket Australia and International Cricket Council (ICC) chief executive—and our ultimate recommendation in 2011 was that both captain and coach be selectors.

There was a strong push from current players, past players and other sports for the coach to have a greater say in the team picked, because he lives and dies on their performances. It makes a lot of sense, and in other sports it would be considered ridiculous for the coach, who has been hired to set the tone and the environment for the team and run the preparation, not to have any say in the selection of players.

Since then, the coach (currently Darren Lehmann) has been a selector. But once we started to go down that path, I felt that the captain was probably even more important than the coach, and that if the coach was a selector then the captain ought to be as well. This was adopted, but Michael Clarke took a different view and stepped down as a selector. He didn't like being seen as a hirer and firer of players as well as the skipper who was trying to engender team spirit, and that thought process is fair enough, too.

Having seen it all work now, I prefer our old system, where the captain isn't a selector but is consulted. I feel that if he's stridently in favour of a certain player, then the selectors should name that player in the team. But it means that within the dressing room, he isn't seen as a hirer and firer, because the four selectors will make the ultimate judgement on performances. In the future, of course, we may have a captain who does want to be a selector. As for Darren Lehmann as coach, he'll now go to the players, or to an individual player, and thrash things out if there are issues.

Nowadays, Cricket Australia always sends a selector on tour in addition to the coach as a selector, so if any player has an issue, that's where he'll go to take it up, rather than to the captain. It's a good system, where Michael Clarke is well respected within the team and in the dressing room: 'He's the boss, but he's not out to get me. I can have a disagreement with him, but it won't affect my position in the team.'

THE ARGUS REPORT brought Pat Howard into the system as general manager of team performance, which is a buck-stopping position. Howard, a former Wallabies rugby union international and highly successful coach, had come from the high performance position with the Wallabies. Australian cricket had reached the stage where if things went wrong (as they did in England in 2005 and 2009), there was finger-pointing and debate about whose fault it was. The coach would say, 'I just coach the side, I don't pick the team.' The manager might say, 'I just manage.' So we made Pat responsible for high performance, and we said, 'If anything goes wrong, we're coming to you.' That's why when the management felt that Mickey Arthur needed to be replaced as head coach in 2013, Pat jumped in and made the change. That's his job.

We tweaked the report here and there. Don Argus would have liked to take it further, but overall I believe the recommendations have been very beneficial. After the Argus report, we hammered it home to the states that the common goal was success for the national team, first and foremost. It's Australia first with all decisions.

We don't want to remove state parochialism, which is part of the strength of our cricket. The states will smash each other on the field, but they should come together afterwards and try to produce 11 good cricketers for Australia. We don't want states corralling players or placing self-interest ahead of national interest.

I think the Argus report served its purpose. Don Argus is a smart guy and he's brought some accountability to our system. In fact, all team sports should do these sorts of reviews every few years, even if they're on top of the world and performing well. They ensure that the system hasn't developed weaknesses that aren't necessarily being reflected on the field.

CRICKET AUSTRALIA IS also undergoing important changes at an administrative level. I'm amazed at how quickly this has happened under Wally Edwards' chairmanship, and it's significant because strong administration tends to filter down.

The board has been trimmed to six directors from the states, plus three independent directors. Previously, the board had 14 state-based directors, but a review of the corporate structure recommended streamlining to a commission-style body like that for the National Rugby League (NRL) and the Australian Football League (AFL). The changes were hailed as the most significant in more than 100 years of the board.

This is as it should be. My only concern is that the board doesn't push too far to the corporate side. I still want ex-players to be involved, and long-term club officials who know how the game works, how to get a fifth-grade team onto the paddock on a Saturday. It's gratifying to me that Mark Taylor, the former Test captain, and Michael Kasprowicz, the former Test fast bowler, remain on the board. It shouldn't just be about the corporate side of the game; it can't be only about the money. It also has to be about the grassroots of the game, and the processes that have worked for Australian cricket for more than a century.

2

Captaincy

MICHAEL CLARKE'S GREATEST strength as captain of Australia is that he doesn't let the game drift. Even if Australia isn't in a dominant position in a game, he'll try to conjure something. He's got this gambler's instinct—he tries to create something to move the game forward. To me, that's a key component of captaincy.

No doubt that can be difficult if you're playing from behind, when you have to stop the rot, rather than focus on creating opportunities. So a lot depends on the cattle you have, but I like Michael for the way he keeps the game moving. He'll confound us sometimes with a declaration. There might be more than two days to play and he declares, but why give the opposition a chance? Then he wins the game easily. He has a feel for those things.

We've been lucky with our captains in recent times. Michael and his predecessors, Steve Waugh and Ricky Ponting, each learnt from the previous skipper but brought their own personalities to the job, introducing their own thought processes and their own strengths.

The important point is that we've had a nice progression, with no kneejerk appointments. I personally struggled with the captaincy for a period, but I like to think I became better at it. Mark Taylor and Steve Waugh followed me and did fantastic jobs, and Ricky Ponting had been in the system for a long time before he got the position. Ricky brought his own style and so does Michael.

The best captains all have their own approach. Steve Waugh, for instance, was excellent with his innovations, he was ruthless and he built up an amazing record. Steve won 41 of 57 Tests from 1999 to 2003–04 and at one point his team won 16 Test matches in a row (of which he captained 15), which was a world record. On statistics, Steve is the best. But having said that, Mark 'Tubby' Taylor (50 Tests, 26 wins) was a brilliant captain who could extract the best from Shane Warne and Glenn McGrath and was tactically top-shelf. Steve inherited a very good team with some superstar players, whereas Ricky Ponting (77 Tests, 48 wins) came to the captaincy nearing the end of that run, which made it more difficult for him, as it became a rebuilding phase.

A good captain will develop strong relationships and loyalties with his players, and I was no different. Over the time I had the job, for 93 Test matches from 1984 to 1994, a lot of young players came into the team and became stars, and I was close with them. Which isn't to say I wasn't hard on them at times.

Frankly, it's about the environment the captain creates. A lot about good captaincy is getting the players to play for you, and in that sense the off-field business is very important. You need the players to respect you as a person and respect the position of captain. They might not always agree with your decisions, but even so, they shouldn't voice it publicly. A captain needs to have that ability to listen and take advice as well, cooperating with his senior players. It's not rocket science. Quite often, the results come down to the quality of players in your team.

I WASN'T A natural captain and I'm not a natural leader. I had to learn as I went. But I hope that the legacy I left helped Mark Taylor to become an outstanding captain as my successor, and Steve Waugh after that as well. We went through tough times when I was first the captain, but we gradually became better and the team evolved. After I left, Australia dominated Test cricket as the No. 1 team for 15 years, and won three consecutive World Cups in one-day cricket. That's the pleasing point for me.

The 'Captain Grumpy' tag came in the mid-eighties, when we were battling as a team. A magazine article that used the headline 'Captain Cranky' might have started it. I can also remember one press conference when we'd lost badly, and Ross Mullins, a journalist from Australian Associated Press, opened the questions with, 'How do you feel, A.B.?' I snapped straight back, 'How the fuck do you *think* I feel, Ross?' Captain Grumpy had arrived!

Being called Captain Grumpy has never bothered me—to be honest, it became a bit of a badge of honour. The players would pick me up if I was annoyed about something—'Look out, Captain Grumpy's back!'—and used it as a joke. I openly admit that I could blow up about things, but I'm the type of person who likes things to work 100 per cent, and if they don't, then I can feel the anger welling up inside.

I did get frustrated, not just with the media but also occasionally with the Australian Cricket Board (ACB, now Cricket Australia). I did at times take matters too seriously, but that's just the way I was. I was reluctant to do the job when the ACB offered the captaincy to me upon Kim Hughes' resignation in 1984 during a home series against the West Indies. I was apprehensive, and not long after that we suffered from the South African split, when Kim led a team to play several series in South Africa while that country was banned from international cricket over its apartheid regime. Our board subsequently suspended those players for three years. Through this period, I lost a lot of confidence in the job. I just didn't know who to trust.

Captaincy

If I wasn't playing well, I hated it. I hated doing dumb things, getting out in stupid ways, and that was when the fuse could blow. I was the same if the team wasn't playing well. Brad Pitt says in the movie *Moneyball*, 'I *hate* losing. I *hate* losing more than I like winning.' I reckon I'm exactly the same. I was motivated by fear of failure. Winning, to me, is just part of a process; if you get your processes right, your preparation is good and your decision-making is good, the outcome is that you win. It's not that I don't *like* winning, but my *expectation* is that you win if you do things right.

GEOFF MARSH'S DROPPING by the selectors during the Test series against India in 1991–92 did upset me. I was loyal to 'Swampy', and he was my vice-captain, a senior player and a great mate. But the selectors chose to drop him four Tests into a five-Test series, and in those days, I had no say in selection. We were 3–0 up in the series and had just won the Adelaide Test, the fourth of the series, to clinch it. We were meant to be having a decent celebration for having beaten a pretty good Indian team, but the news that Geoff wouldn't be playing the final Test in Perth, his home town, ruined the atmosphere.

Granted, Swampy was struggling with the bat. He'd made eight and five in that Adelaide match, but he was a popular member of the team and we'd won the series.

I thought he was entitled to some leeway. I was very disappointed, and not for selfish reasons—I couldn't see the logic of it, four Tests into a series. As a result of Geoff's axing, Victorian Wayne Phillips was selected to open the batting for the Test match in Perth.

If the selectors had explained to me the reasons for their decision, it might have helped my mood. But from memory it was the coach, Bob Simpson, who told me on the last day of the Adelaide Test, and I spat the dummy. I wanted answers. I decided to ring Laurie Sawle, the chairman of selectors, to put my case.

That phone call took place while play was going on, which meant that Paul Reiffel, the 12th man, had to go out on the field. Of course, 'Pistol' had no idea what was going on, but when he came out of the shower I had the shits, so I told him to get his whites on. I wasn't letting this go. Geoff Marsh was a long-term player and good friend. I was a bit blinkered, but why not tap him on the shoulder and say, 'It's been good, Swampy, but we're going to move on. You've got the Perth Test to finish. You can announce it.' I didn't even go to Perth that night with the team, which the media picked up on. I stayed behind, had a few beers.

Wayne Phillips had been a good player for Victoria. When I got word that he wasn't going to be selected for the tour of Sri Lanka straight after Perth, that made me angrier. What was the point of picking Wayne Phillips for one Test in Perth? If Wayne was going on to Sri Lanka then fine, he's away with the boys and he gets the extended chance to prove himself. But he didn't win selection for Sri Lanka, and Perth ended up being his one and only Test for Australia.

At that time, we'd reached a period where our team ethos was strong. We'd won the World Cup in 1987, won the Ashes in 1989 in England, and beaten England again in the summer of 1990–91. We were rebuilding, and that's why I was so disappointed. Geoff Marsh had been part of that process, but he never played another Test match. We're all big boys, and we know we won't be playing forever, but no one came to me and said, 'What do you think about Swampy? He's struggling.' Had that happened, I might have taken it better.

KIM HUGHES WAS a fine player and a fine person, and it impacted on me, the way he lost the captaincy in 1984, resigning in tears at the Gabba during a Test match against the West Indies when they were at their mightiest. I felt for him. I was his vice-captain. What happened to Kim, the way the pressure of the captaincy got to him, was one of the main reasons I was so reluctant to take over.

We'd played ten consecutive Test matches against the West Indians—five in the Caribbean and then five at home over the summer of 1984–85. As a piece of scheduling it won't go down as one of the ACB's finest moments.

The West Indies were an awesome team with the best battery of fast bowlers anyone had ever seen, and it hit Kim hard.

We lost in the West Indies, 3–0, and Kim only averaged 21.50 for the series. It was relentless. They went after him, as captain, and his plan was to counterattack. He got out hooking a few times, and whereas his idea of not taking a backward step had worked for him in some previous series, this time it was unsuccessful. The wear and tear got to him. Then for some crazy reason we played the first Test of the home series in Perth, on the quick, bouncy WACA Ground strip. Whatever happened to putting them on a nice SCG turner first up? We lost by an innings at the WACA and then went on to Brisbane, another less than ideal venue to play against Malcolm Marshall, Joel Garner and Courtney Walsh. We lost badly again at the Gabba, went 2–0 down, and Kim hit the wall.

Kim was a seriously good player, and courageous. Unfortunately, when a lot of people think about Kim's cricket, the 'tearful resignation' comes to mind, but we need to remember that he was really good. He was an entertainer and always wanted the game to be moving. He wasn't an accumulator, grinding out a score for the red ink. If the game was dragging along and heading for a draw, he'd try to hit six sixes in an over and probably get out, but he was as tough as they come, and he wasn't soft. I'll never forget some of his innings against the West Indies in that period:

a hundred he made in Brisbane in 1979–80 and the unbelievable ton he extracted at the MCG in 1981–82, where we won. People are inclined to forget the innings Kim played that day (100 not out of 198 all out), because Dennis Lillee took a stack of brilliant wickets at the end. But it was Kim who set it up.

The game got him, the system got him. He felt he was being undermined behind the scenes, so I think it's understandable that he broke down as he tried to read out his resignation speech at the Gabba that day. Kim had been the captain of the Test side in the WSC days, when the main players were with the Packer series. When the reconciliation happened, Kim stood aside for Greg Chappell to take over, although when Greg didn't take the Ashes tour in 1981, Kim stepped in again. He didn't captain a full Australian team on what you'd call an established basis until 1983, and not long after that we played the West Indies for ten Tests in a row.

I was always a big supporter of Kim, and I do remember him coming to me that day in Brisbane when we were in the throes of losing. He said, 'A.B., I want to have a quick chat.' We left the dressing room and he handed me a piece of paper as he said, 'What do you think of this?' It was his resignation note. I said, 'Mate, what are you doing? It's not your fault we're outgunned. The West Indies are a pretty good team. We support you, we just need to play better.' He said, 'I've had enough. I'm not enjoying the game.'

I know he felt he was having sand shovelled from under his feet, and his form with the bat had suffered—he'd averaged just 10.12 in the four Tests of that series before missing the fifth match.

The statement Kim showed to me that day read:

The Australian Cricket Captaincy is something that I've held very dear to me. However playing the game with total enjoyment has always been of the greatest importance. The constant speculation, criticism and inuendo [*sic*] by former players and sections of the media over the past 4–5 years have finally taken their toll. It is in the interests of the team, Australian Cricket and myself that I have informed the ACB of my decision to stand down as Australian Captain. I look forward to continuing my career in whichever capacity the selectors and the Board see fit with the same integrity and credability [*sic*] I have displayed as Australian captain.

I talked to Kim about his position on the day, but needless to say I couldn't talk him round. Of course it was a huge story in the media, the dramatic resignation of an Australian captain. Some commentators mocked Kim for his tears; others were sympathetic, such as Bill Lawry: 'The demise of Kim Hughes in Brisbane in a manner equal to being dragged down like a dingo in the pack and devoured by your own, within and without, was a disgrace.' Hughes made two and a duck in the next Test match in Adelaide, then a pair of ducks including a first-baller in Melbourne. He was exhausted, and never played Test cricket again.

Kim had first played for Australia on the 1977 Ashes tour, which happened to be when the news of the WSC defections broke, although initially the implications weren't especially clear. He played one Test under Greg Chappell's captaincy before the Packer matches were formulated and the camps were divided. Hughes, who stood in the establishment camp, issued a statement that made his position clear: 'It is completely understandable that players approaching retirement or even past players should avail themselves of an opportunity to capitalise on their skills. The necessity for all young players—and we do have some brilliant ones knocking on the door—is to dedicate, train long and hard . . . That's what I propose to do. That's exactly where I stand.'

While he wasn't an immediate success, he broke into the team and was elevated to the captaincy in just his 11th Test match, at Perth in 1978–79 against Pakistan, when Graham Yallop was injured. He captained Australia at the World Cup in England in 1979, then on two tours Greg Chappell declined, and by the summer of 1983–84, he was the captain of Australia on a formal basis for the tour by Pakistan, as the triumvirate of Chappell, Dennis Lillee and Rod Marsh bade farewell to the game. This was the somewhat threadbare team Kim would have to take forward.

A FEW DAYS after Kim Hughes stepped down at the Gabba, it started to hit home to me that as the vice-captain, I might be asked to lead the team. There were still three Test matches to play against the touring West Indians, starting in Adelaide, but in the meantime we all headed off to play Sheffield Shield cricket and I broke a finger batting against the Tasmanian quick Roger Brown. It was a bouncer and it snapped a bone in the little finger of my top hand, so here I was, about to captain Australia for the first time, playing against the most fearsome bowling attack you could imagine, and I had a quite serious hand injury. Needless to say, the timing wasn't ideal. I had to wear a guard on that finger for months, and it was painful. I had to have that finger not quite gripping the handle, which was a little uncomfortable when I batted.

Nothing had been said to me at any official level about the captaincy, and I'd started to toss it around in my head when David Richards, the ACB's chief executive, asked for a meeting with me on the way home from the Tasmanian Shield game. We met at a hotel near Tullamarine airport for some talks and he offered me the captaincy. To put it bluntly, I was very reluctant. I thought Kim should have kept going, and it wasn't something I'd ever considered before he stepped down. I didn't want to dance on Kim's grave. I liked and respected him very much.

Vice-captain in those days was in some ways a decorative position. There was no actual job at all, other than being one of the senior players. It's since evolved into an important role in the modern game. Now you're the sergeant major; the captain has his duties but you're in the trenches with the troops. It's not the captain who jumps on the back of players about discipline; it's probably the vice-captain. That's changed with professional thinking, but back in 1984 I was still just one of the boys.

I saw what the captaincy had done to Kim and I was very comfortable being one of the team, scoring as many runs as I could. There's a certain amount of freedom in just being an individual in a team. With the captaincy, you're in the spotlight, and I've always felt uncomfortable in the spotlight. This clouded my thoughts initially. 'Why would you want to do this job? Who wants to captain the team against the West Indies every day? You'd have to be a masochist! There has to be a joy in playing.'

It's not a good mindset to go in with. When Michael Clarke was appointed in 2011, he'd been one of the boys and had probably reached the point where he wanted to take it a level further. He had some time to get his head around that situation, because he'd been playing at Test level for seven years. But in my case, it was a shock to see Kim go. I hadn't even been in the role of vice-captain very long, although I'd captained Queensland a few times because Greg Chappell had stepped aside and wanted me to do it. You do get to a point where the leadership might become attractive, and perhaps in time, if Kim had captained for another couple of series, I might have started to think, 'I wouldn't mind a crack at this.' But I definitely hadn't reached that point.

Ultimately, of course, I didn't say no. A small part of me was excited, and a big part was reluctant. My first press conference was at Melbourne airport, in the departure lounge, and my tone on the day probably reveals some of my thought process: 'I'd just like to point out that I've been a little disappointed at the circumstances surrounding my appointment,' I said, 'but I'd like to go on record as saying it's a great honour and I can just assure everyone that I'll give it 100 per cent and do my best.'

There are two parts of the captaining equation for me: one is the on-field captaincy, the 'who bowls where and when'; and the other is the off-field leadership, the creation of an environment. To be honest, I came round to thinking, 'Who else is going to do it? Who can they pick to captain the team who's going to be around for a period of time, someone with some longevity?' You don't want four captains in a series, where someone comes in and comes crashing down. In Australia, we've been pretty strong with our 'pick and stick' policy with captains. Most guys have had a good run at it, and they've been given some leeway with their own form because they've deserved it. I was that player then, but who else was there? I got the captaincy a bit by default, if you like, and I was reluctant. But I could have said no. Once I took it on, I enjoyed it, although that took a few years to kick in.

MY FIRST THREE Tests as captain were against the West Indies, and it all began in Adelaide. Kim had started a tradition of having a guest from the sporting world at our main team meeting before a Test match, which had worked quite well and we found helpful. Someone like Kevin Sheedy, the AFL coach, would come in and mingle with us, not necessarily lecture us. When I arrived in Adelaide, it had already been arranged that Sir Donald Bradman would be our guest.

I was already nervous about the captaincy, talking publicly isn't one of my great strengths, and then I had Sir Donald sitting there listening in. It was quite daunting, but he was great. He wasn't required to make a speech but inevitably the guys started asking him questions and it evolved into a little session. Someone asked Sir Donald how long he'd use a bat for, and he said, 'I'd get a thousand or so runs out of a bat.' Then John Dyson piped up with, 'Well, that's just a couple of knocks, then!'

We had a good night. We talked about Bodyline, and its similarities to facing the West Indian quicks. Sir Donald said he understood how difficult it was with four fast bowlers coming at you, whereas with Bodyline there was pace bowling, but it was more about the fielding positions, with the packed leg-side field that was made illegal sometime after that 1932–33 series. I think we all came away feeling better about ourselves, in the sense that if the greatest player of all time understood how difficult the task was we were confronting, then perhaps other people would, too. What hit home was that he was very current; he didn't talk about Harold Larwood being better than Malcolm Marshall. He was a very keen observer of the game.

We lost in Adelaide, drew in Melbourne and won in Sydney, spinning them out on an SCG turner. We'd copped a battering for months and we ended on a high, but I always remember that when I tossed with their captain Clive Lloyd, the ground staff had left the wicket a bit tacky, making it a tricky call, especially for an inexperienced captain.

Steve 'Stumper' Rixon was in the side as keeper and he said beforehand, 'A.B., you have to bat first because this will turn.' The team had been picked accordingly, with Murray Bennett and the 38-year-old Bob 'Dutchy' Holland there to bowl spin. But it did look like a bowl-first wicket. When I won the toss and I said, 'We'll bat,' Clive Lloyd half-giggled. He was comfortable, and I'm sure he would have elected to bowl anyway. For the first hour or so, it was a nightmare for the top order, and Andrew Hilditch went early. We somehow got to lunch only one wicket down, then Kepler Wessels (who ended up making 173) and Graeme Wood came in and they were into me: 'What the fuck are you doing? It's a nightmare out there.' I said, 'Sorry boys, but it's going to turn.'

I went to Steve Rixon and said, 'Stumper, this wicket better fucking turn.' He said, 'A.B., trust me, it'll turn.' We all chipped in to grind out a good score, 471, and Kepler was fantastic. When we bowled, Murray Bennett's first ball pitched and spun a mile and I remember looking at Stumper. He had this big grin on his face, and I knew we had them. We won by an innings, Dutchy took 10 wickets and Bennett bowled Viv Richards with a memorable arm ball. Just three Tests into my captaincy we had a win, a loss and a draw and I could feel some new energy in the team.

I CHANGED A bit in my first few years as captain, just with the pressure. Certain issues affected me personally, and I became more guarded, a lot grumpier! It was a big job and, as I've said, I wasn't ready. It affected me more than I realised at the time. In 1985, when we were due to tour England for an Ashes series, an Australian 'rebel' tour of South Africa was announced, with Kim Hughes as captain. Ultimately, this would mean that a few key players would miss the Ashes tour. South Africa was banned from international cricket at the time over the apartheid regime, although there had been several English rebel tours.

It came as a complete shock to me. It was a matter of weeks before we left for England and I was up at Noosa Heads with the family and a mate having a break. My eldest son, Dene, was only one year old, and we were with family friends. Life was good and then, one morning, I heard on the radio at breakfast about the tour of South Africa with seven of the players who'd been picked for England. I can remember that during the 1983 World Cup in England there were rumours of a rebel tour by Australians, but nothing concrete had occurred until this time. We bolted down to the newsagent and read the story. There were no mobile phones in those days, but the phone in the apartment started running hot. It was pretty traumatic.

Bob Hawke, the prime minister, called them 'traitors', and lambasted them for the decision to tour a country that was a pariah at the time. He said, 'On the issue of South Africa and sporting contact with South Africa, I and this government won't change our view about that obnoxious system of apartheid. We won't change our position as to it being not right for people to collect themselves and deem themselves an Australian team, to give aid and comfort to that regime in South Africa . . . which is so blatantly and desperately seeking international legitimacy via the medium of apparent international competition.'

As I said, all this unfolded only a few weeks before we flew to England. New players had been added to the touring team. We'd gathered in Melbourne and there'd been a lot of activity. Four of our team for England had been persuaded to back out of contracts they'd signed to go to South Africa. Our understanding was that Kerry Packer, head of Channel Nine, had cherrypicked the ones he wanted to remain in the 'establishment' fold with us and induced them to change their minds. The South African tourists were getting $200,000 each; for our England tour most of the guys would have been getting about $16,000.

At first, I was extremely disappointed with the players who had signed to go to South Africa. I felt that we were really starting to get a good, solid group together. The initial side that had been picked to travel to England, I felt, had a huge chance of bringing home the Ashes. All that was unravelling. Then, to further compound the issue, four players were apparently getting paid big bucks to back out of the rebel tour.

My big issue was with those four—Graeme Wood, Murray Bennett, Wayne Phillips and Dirk Wellham—and they had to face a 'kangaroo court' convened by the rest of the playing group. The boys started firing questions at them: 'Are you getting paid more?' 'Are you with us or against us?' As it turned out, Murray Bennett had dropped out of the South African tour on conscience a long time before the Ashes squad had been named, so we felt he was fine to tour. At the time, I'd been getting phone calls from players who were going to South Africa, and they were even angrier with those four, now three, players than we were. It was said to me, 'You were the captain, we knew you wouldn't go, and it would've got out of the bag if you'd been invited.' So it was all done under solidarity: 'They'll come at us really hard, but we've got to stay strong.' So they were angry that three had dropped out, and not for reasons of conscience.

In the end, all but one of us voted against them touring England with us. We wanted the board to pick three other players, and I delivered that decision to Fred Bennett, the ACB chairman, and Bob Merriman, another board member who was to manage the team in England. I said, 'We don't want to go with these blokes. We're not sure they're committed to us. We want a fresh, clean slate.'

The board wouldn't accept it. They said, 'Allan, the deal's been done. They're going on the tour.' They also said something like: 'If you have dramas when you're over there, you have our permission to send them home.' I was thinking, 'You're kidding, aren't you? I'm going to make that decision as captain in England? You guys have to make the decision now.' In the end, the three remained and we just got on with the job.

I never held a grudge against the guys who went to South Africa, but initially I felt let down and betrayed. Time heals most wounds, and I'm relaxed about all that now. I can understand 80 per cent of them going to South Africa, because $200,000 was a lot of money, and quite a few of them had little or no chance of playing for Australia. You could never say that Trevor Hohns shouldn't have done it, for instance. It actually made him a better cricketer, and after the three-year ban was served, he came back and played for Australia as a leg-spinner. Steve Smith, the opening batsman, was a big loss, and so were Terry Alderman, Carl Rackemann and Rodney Hogg. Kim Hughes had been dropped, so I had no issue with him going, but I lost faith in the board at that time, and our results were poor. We suffered for the absence of players and we were still getting over the retirements of the three greats—Greg Chappell, Dennis Lillee and Rod Marsh.

Now, when I think about Carl Rackemann, who was injured a lot, and 'Clem' Alderman, who'd also been injured, I understand. They had a guaranteed two years of cricket and $200,000 to set themselves up or buy a business. Maybe I was looking through rose-coloured glasses, but to have that happen and not know anything about it, I felt betrayed, especially as we'd just started to turn our cricket around. But I do remember how I'd walk into a bar and the conversation would stop. I might not have thought anything about it at the time, but looking back it was an uncomfortable feeling. The earliest instance was one night at the 1983 World Cup, when three or four guys said, after I'd suggested going for a feed, 'We've got something else organised.' Now I think about it, I guess they were going to see someone to talk about South Africa.

I'd had a conversation with Kepler Wessels about South Africa much earlier, long before any rebel tours were announced. Kepler, of course, had come out of South Africa to play for Australia in WSC in 1978, and then for the full Australian Test team. He asked me if I'd ever go to South Africa on a tour, and I said, 'No way.' My feeling came about because the board had been saying, 'If you go to South Africa, you'll be banned for life. That's it.' I wasn't thinking so much about the ethics of going to South Africa; I didn't want to be banned from playing for my country.

I wasn't worldly enough to get involved in the protests against the apartheid regime, or any of the politics. For me, it was pragmatism. I said, 'I don't care what they'd pay me. I want to play cricket for Australia.' Having made it very clear I wasn't interested, I was never asked again, and Kim was originally the same. He didn't know about the plans either, but when he was left out of the touring team to England, they targeted him. We all made our decisions in the end. It was always there in the background in 1985, that feeling in the team that some were earning more money. When the bans were announced by the state associations, they were only two years, although we'd initially heard that they'd be longer.

The 1985 tour of England was actually an enjoyable one in the end. The spirit was good, but the wheels fell off in the last few weeks. We set the South African situation aside as best we could and got on with playing. It wasn't the ideal start, but we were playing England, and if you can't get up for that, then something's drastically wrong. We won at Lord's but lost our way in the last month and lost the Ashes.

Then Richard Hadlee wiped us out in 1985–86. On a tour of New Zealand in 1986 I was close to quitting the captaincy. I started to think, 'Maybe it's me. The boys aren't responding to me.' We were playing badly, I got frustrated and I blurted out at a press conference, 'Maybe it's time for me to give it away if I don't have the support.' I was in a bad headspace. It clouded the way I captained the team and I wasn't really grabbing hold of the job and making it happen. The team had a meeting without me at that time and told me they wanted me to go on. The whole thing bubbled and then died a slow death.

That's when the cricket board brought Bob Simpson into the fold, initially as cricket manager, and then later as coach, which was effectively the same thing. It wasn't something I sought or asked for, but it was good for me, no doubt. Simmo injected a bit of steel and led the preparation of the team, which meant I could relax just a little and do what I needed to do. It's remarkable to think that back then most international cricket teams didn't have a coach.

I'd played with Simmo in the days of the WSC split, as a young bloke for New South Wales. We had a good relationship, and he became the sergeant major, the disciplinarian;

he was very strict about our work ethic, and he put a structure in place for the way we went about things. Until then, the Australian captain had basically been all things. We had a manager, but a lot of it fell on the captain, and we were doing a lot of travelling and playing one-day cricket. The game had changed. I'm not saying that a good, strong captain couldn't have done it, but at the time Simmo was just a good bloke to have around to instil the work ethic. I let him do his thing and I was still the captain, but I could do things better with him handling practices and discipline and the nitty-gritty.

Slowly but surely we were gathering a proper management group around the team. We picked up Errol Alcott as physiotherapist on the 1984 West Indies tour and he stayed for more than 20 years. Whereas board members had taken it in turns as team manager, Ian McDonald now came to do that job permanently. We had good people involved, and I bounced tactics off Simmo as well as taking his ideas on board. But I wasn't the finished article as a captain at that point and the team itself wasn't particularly stable.

Selection was quite hit and miss in those times, with blokes coming in and out. The South African tourists were suspended, and a lot of guys were playing for their place in the team. We hadn't reached that 'pick and stick' philosophy, which can be pretty difficult without the right blokes at your disposal. At times, you give guys an opportunity and they're not up to it, so what do you do? You can't just stick with them forever. But you also need the courage to pick guys you think will have some longevity.

Unless he's injured, I'm against the idea of giving a guy just one chance. Don't pick a guy and say, 'We're not sure but let's give him a go.' You're trying to create an environment where everyone's happy and comfortable and away you go. That's where Darren Lehmann has been so good in the past year. It sounds simplistic, but it's the way to go, because if you chop and change, everyone's inclined to look after number one, rather than think about the collective. Cricket *is* a game where you look after number one, but you do it within the team scenario. If you have 11 selfish players, you won't win many games. You might win games on talent, but you'll eventually get your comeuppance. Good, solid groups find a way to win at those big moments.

ALL THIS TURNED in the summer of 1986–87, ironically with a really bad defeat. I remember the exact moment. We'd lost the Ashes series at home, horrendously so. We fell over in three days in the Fourth Test at Melbourne, and at 2–0 down the Ashes had already gone. England held the Ashes from their 1985 win, and Mike Gatting's team was dominating us. We made only 141 and 194 in Melbourne, and it completed a 14th Test in a row without a win. I've heard people say this might be an all-time low for Australian cricket, and it's hard to argue.

In the MCG dressing rooms after the match was over, we were feeling sorry for ourselves. The Davis Cup tennis final was on down the road at Kooyong on the grass, and Pat Cash was playing Mikael Pernfors of Sweden. We sat there watching the tennis on television and having a few beers. The England boys were there and barracking for Sweden, and Pernfors was two sets to love up, but 'Cashy' ground it out in a famous victory. We were jumping up and down; it gave us a real lift.

Then Bob Hawke as prime minister, who was part of the presentation of the Davis Cup, came on and said, 'It's a pity there weren't more Pat Cashes at the MCG today!' Cans and rubbish were thrown at the television but the bottom line was that Hawke was probably justified. We got together in Ian McDonald's room that night at the Hilton—it would have been me, David Boon, Geoff Marsh, Dean Jones and a few others—and it was one of those nights where you draw a line. We made a pact: 'We've gone as low as we can go. There's only one way to go from here.'

IT WASN'T JUST about the team turning the corner, it was about me as captain, too. We won the World Cup in India and Pakistan in 1987 against all expectations, which was one of the great moments for us, and in England in 1989 we retrieved the Ashes, once again to the surprise of many.

Captaincy

I took a different mindset into the captaincy, even if it was a long time coming. I was a lot more proactive with field placings and the way I set things up. There are probably two parts to my ten years as the skipper: five years of battling with it and five years of good times and being more creative. In England in 1989, I made a conscious decision to put a harder edge into the way we played the game. I'd been on two previous Ashes tours and had my backside kicked, so I thought, 'Enough's enough! We have to toughen up.'

I gave some thought to the way we'd approached previous tours and the distractions for the players. The upshot was that we discouraged the wives from being with the team—a controversial and difficult decision. We had a team meeting, and I pushed my case. In 1981 and 1985 the wives and girlfriends had arrived early in the tour; some of them were in the team hotel and some weren't. I sold the idea of us being together in a tight group for the first six weeks or so, which meant no wives would be allowed in the hotel. It was portrayed as 'no wives on tour' but they were around; they just couldn't stay at our hotel.

I was mindful of keeping the group together. The players could go off and spend time with their partners when they were free, but they had to spend the night at the team hotel and there was trouble if they were found to be breaking that edict. It sounds like I was dealing with schoolboys, but it was designed to bring the group together with a common purpose. Jane, my wife, wasn't there. She stayed at home in Brisbane with two youngsters and it was tough, because we were away for five months. But I felt I needed to set the example if I was going to make the rules.

I copped a bit from the wives and the players, but that side gelled. Maybe it would have happened anyway: that's the million-dollar question. The women did confront me later on, saying, 'It can't be our fault if you don't play well.' I just said, 'From past experience, I just wanted the side together. I didn't want any distractions. I wanted to create a group that was going in the same direction.' It's just a percentage thing. Some guys like to have their wives there, and it's an issue, but with this group I just got lucky. They understood where I was coming from, and although they didn't all necessarily agree with it, they went along with it. Then the wives started to trickle in, and because we were doing well, we were relaxed.

We did most things together on that trip. We had appearances to make at pubs, because we were sponsored by XXXX. When we played the counties in the past, they'd been glorified practice games, and I wanted to change that. I wanted to play the counties like we were playing a proper match, and if someone was on 90 and we wanted to declare, then I'd declare. We tried to win; we didn't just practise, which was a subtle change of mindset, and it worked. We'd been greeted by the usual 'worst Australian touring team ever' headlines, so it wasn't hard to motivate the team.

Captaincy

We played positive, aggressive cricket, we tried to win, and the team came first in decision-making.

I also stayed with the team, even when I wasn't playing. On the 1985 tour, when I'd had a chance to have two or three days off during a county game, I'd taken it, gone away to London with Jane, played some golf and had some fun. But invariably I found that I'd come back to some little spot fire, so on the 1989 tour I stayed around the whole time. The reality is that the captain needs to be right there in case anything gets out of hand.

I sat down with Terry Alderman, Geoff Lawson and Merv Hughes before the 1989 tour and we made some plans for the England batsmen. With Graham Gooch, I'd noticed that he fell across the line and hit in the air sometimes, so we went with a bat-pad and a short mid-wicket. Clem managed to get him lbw so many times in that series, and we got into his head. Gooch was a great player but he only averaged 20.33 in that series. Similarly, Geoff Lawson had noticed that David Gower would fall away to cover his off stump and then flick the ball backward of square, so we put a leg slip in place. We dismissed him with that on the last day of the First Test at Leeds.

We were ruthless and the English guys didn't like it. They were taken aback because I'd been quite tight with some of them, like Graham Gooch, Ian Botham and David Gower, but if it meant a friendship went, I was prepared to wear it. I wasn't nasty to them, but I turned more of a cold shoulder, and I didn't talk to them as much or spend as much time with them.

It was difficult to do that, because Gower was their captain, and I had to walk out to toss with him at every Test match. But I didn't go to the English rooms once that series, and we were nowhere near as tight as we'd been with the opposition. We'd be far from the first or last to take a harder line at a particular time, because I can remember England playing the same way in 2005. The first ball of that series hit Justin Langer a nasty blow and he was hurt, but no Englishman went to him to see if he was okay. They were sick and tired of losing and they'd made up their minds to go harder. They also won that series.

So in 1989 I think David Gower, as captain, was most affected by it, because we were friends. It caught him on the hop a bit, and he said to me, 'You've turned into a grumpy old bastard.' I said, 'Fair point,' but I did what I thought I had to do. By tour's end, the scoreline read 4–0 to Australia and the Ashes were won.

3

The Twenty20 revolution

I CALL THE arrival of Twenty20 the second revolution of cricket. The first was Kerry Packer's World Series Cricket, the big split in the game in 1977. As head of Channel Nine, Packer wanted to buy the television rights for cricket, but the Australian Cricket Board at the time wanted to remain with the ABC, which had held the rights for years. Packer tried big financial inducements but they wouldn't budge, so Packer set up his own matches to televise on Channel Nine, and signed most of the best players in the world.

The Chappells, Dennis Lillee, Rod Marsh and the top Australians signed with Packer's WSC, and I can understand why. The Packer revolution was good for the game; it had to happen. Cricket was no longer a pastime where blokes played for fun and had to have a job and think about their families and their careers as they approached their late twenties. One day the inevitable happened and someone thought, 'Hang on, there are 50,000 people here at the game. I wonder where all the money goes?' The Kerry Packer revolution took what was basically an amateur sport and professionalised it. I think the second revolution is fine as well, for reasons I'll explain here.

Twenty20 wasn't around when I was playing, of course, although there was an inkling of it. The Hong Kong Sixes was around and is still going strong, as were other short versions of the game. In 1992 and for a few years afterwards, we played a third-generation game called Super Eights in Hong Kong, Australia and Kuala Lumpur, Malaysia. It was fun, a match lasted only about two hours, and it was popular, but for whatever reason it never took off in the way Twenty20 did.

Martin Crowe, the former New Zealand captain, also had a concept called Cricket Max, which he invented in 1996. Crowe was on the right track. It was two sets of ten overs for each team, quite similar to the modern Twenty20 game, and his spiel at the time sounds very familiar: 'There is far more scoring than ever before and also the potential for electric defensive work in the field. Cricket Max can be played and watched by anyone but nothing can beat seeing the best in the world display their skills in a whole match in just 3 hours.' For some unaccountable reason, it bobbled along but never exploded in popularity. Perhaps the world wasn't ready.

The Twenty20 revolution

Around that time, people had started to examine the more traditional 50-overs-a-side one-day cricket, and they could see that teams had found a way to take some of the risk out of batting through the middle overs, when opposing teams tended to place the field out on the boundary. One-day international cricket had been around since the seventies, and of course the players and coaches had found ways to get better at it. Unfortunately, that also led to some games that were a bit boring, particularly in those middle overs. The authorities had tried the concept of the power-play, where batting and fielding teams could choose to have fielding restrictions changed for a set period, but this hadn't proven especially successful. And so people started coming up with alternative genres of the game.

Then Twenty20 suddenly took off, initially in England at county level. The England and Wales Cricket Board (ECB) had dropped one of its limited-overs competitions, the Benson & Hedges Cup, and wanted another competition to replace it. Stuart Robertson, marketing manager of the ECB, is the man credited with 'inventing' Twenty20 cricket in 2001. Robertson and the ECB were perturbed by falling crowds at county cricket, and invested huge sums in market research before coming up with the solution. 'We spent £200,000, which was considered to be a lot of money for something like this,' Robertson told the *Daily Mail*. 'We tried to identify who was coming to cricket matches but, more importantly, who wasn't and why. There was a significant decline in attendances across the board and we had to do something about it. We came up with something that we hoped would appeal to people who were cash-rich but time-poor.'

The notion wasn't universally popular, which might seem ironic now. Seven counties voted against the proposal when it was first put to the ECB, but the 11 that voted yes got the proposal through and the rest is history. They created a Twenty20 competition for the counties in 2003 and big crowds immediately started turning out. Plainly, people liked the fact that the game was done and dusted in three hours. There were big crowds and *new* crowds, people who had never witnessed a cricket match of any sort before. Cricket authorities couldn't help but notice the vibe as a sellout 15,000 crowd watched Surrey beat Warwickshire in the first season's final at Trent Bridge, Nottingham. 'Don't ask us, you just have to look at the crowds—they are the judge of whether something is a good product or not,' Surrey's captain Adam Hollioake said, summing up the feeling.

Cricket had a new commercial vehicle and it was a streamlined model. The next season, Lord's hosted the final and 27,000 people turned out to see Middlesex meet Surrey, the biggest crowd for a county game of any sort since the fifties. By then, cricket boards around the world were already making plans to copy what was happening in England. Australia's first Twenty20 domestic competition was launched in January 2005, with a sellout 20,000 crowd in Perth watching Western Australia play Victoria. The gates were closed half an hour after the start of the match. Ultimately, this would morph into the Big Bash League, where the original state-based competition was replaced by eight franchises, based in the capital cities, with teams such as the Brisbane Heat and Perth Scorchers.

Initially, cricket authorities were unsure whether Twenty20 cricket was best played as an international game or a domestic competition. The ICC held its first Twenty20 World Cup in 2007, won by India. It was a significant moment in cricket history, as up until that point India had vigorously opposed the new format. The inaugural Women's Twenty20 World Cup was played in 2009. From then on, the competition would be played every two years, but the domestic competitions that had sprung up around the world were just as popular. Ireland, Scotland and the Netherlands could be very competitive in Twenty20 cricket down the track, and I can see them knocking over the traditional countries. The Pepsi Indian Premier League, which started in 2008, has been the most popular and lucrative for the players. The IPL's brand value was estimated at $4 billion in 2010 and in 2014 is around $3 billion. It's a phenomenon.

The players are the big winners. In the annual auction for IPL marquee players in 2014, India's Yuvraj Singh extracted $2.3 million, keeper-batsman Dinesh Karthik

also went for more than $2 million, and two Austra-
lians, Glenn Maxwell and Mitchell Johnson, both topped
$1 million, with David Warner close behind. If you look
further down the list of contracted players, you'll find the
likes of Nathan Coulter-Nile, a talented but as yet unfulfilled Australian fast bowler and hard-hitting batsman
earning more than $700,000. Brad Hodge, the Victorian
batsman who retired from first-class cricket a few years
ago, drew $400,000. And no wonder Mike Hussey has
kept playing beyond his retirement from the international
game: his contract at Mumbai Indians was more than
$800,000.

Now this is for six or seven weeks of cricket! It's
astonishing and, needless to say, it's changed the cricket
landscape forever.

I QUITE LIKE Twenty20 cricket, even though deep down I'm
a Test cricket guy. Twenty20 cricket is pure entertainment.
It's the music, the dancers, the razzamatazz. It's not just
about cricket, and it brings new spectators, new sponsors
and a new television audience to the game, as well as new
skills for the players. We see incredible power-hitting now,
the fielding has improved, the bowling tactics are evolving.
I like it for what it is, although for me it's not the sport of
cricket per se. I don't take much notice of averages and
numbers, although that will change with time, but I do

My first tour of India and the subcontinent was in 1979, under Kim
Hughes as captain. It was the first time Australia had been back there
for a decade, and it was a much tougher place to tour then than it is now.
This was the Sixth Test, at Bombay, and the sixth Test we failed to win
in the series, going down 2–0. (Adrian Murrell/Allsport/Getty Images)

The 1981 Ashes are often called 'Botham's Ashes', but fortunately Botham
failed to catch me off Bob Willis's bowling on this occasion. It was
the First Test at Trent Bridge, Nottingham—the only Test we won in the
series—on my first full tour of England. He got me caught and bowled
instead. (Bob Thomas/Getty Images)

The 1985 Ashes, my first tour of England as captain, was difficult, as several players had chosen to tour South Africa instead. In the Second Test at Lord's, Gatting helped me on my way to 196 when he caught the ball in his stomach but it somehow popped out. Botham got me later, but we did win the match. (Adrian Murrell/Allsport UK/Getty Images)

In England's first innings of the Fifth Test, Gower made 215 before finally being dismissed. I had been going pretty well with the bat, so I think Richard Ellison was glad to get me out for two in the second innings. England won the series 3–1.
(Adrian Murrell/Getty Images)

In the final of the 1987 World Cup at Kolkata, I was lucky enough to capture Mike Gatting's wicket when he tried a reverse sweep shot. This is one of two dismissals he still gets ribbed about by any Australian who meets him. (Adrian Murrell/Getty Images)

Dean Jones and Craig McDermott decided to parade me round the ground holding the World Cup. It was the start of a much better time for the Australian team, and we went on to win our next Test series, against New Zealand. (Getty Images)

I was doing some press interviews by the pool the day after our win in the World Cup. The boys thought it would be hilarious to throw me in the pool mid-sentence. (Bob Thomas/Getty Images)

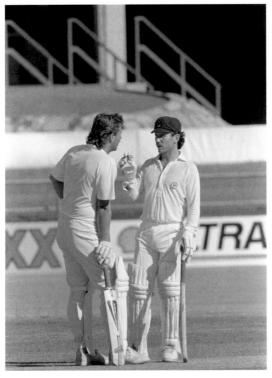

How things change. In 1987–88 Botham joined the Queensland Sheffield Shield team and we played on the same side for once. (Adrian Murrell/Allsport UK)

Boxing Day Test, 1988: Watching the Windies hit balls to the MCG fence is no fun—Viv Richards doesn't waste time. We lost this match by 285 runs and the series 3–1. (Tony Feder/Getty Images)

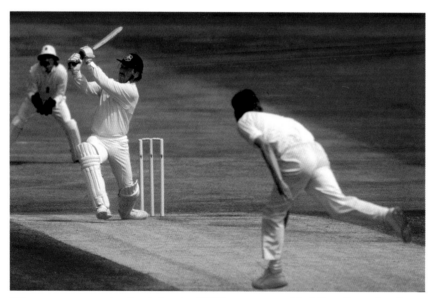

We were out to win the Ashes in 1989—no more Mr Nice Guys. In the First Test at Headingley, Leeds, in June, Steve Waugh made 177 not out in the first innings, Terry Alderman took ten wickets, and we were on our way. (Patrick Eagar/Getty Images)

After the win in the First Test, we had to celebrate. With David Boon in the dressing room you're guaranteed there will be some beers consumed.
(Adrian Murrell/Getty Images)

Terry Alderman's figures showed our new bowling approach was working. Part of the key to the change in the team, though, was Simmo, who had come on as our coach in 1986.

In the 1989 Ashes I had a much more steely approach to the opposition, even my old mate David Gower. He was always an elegant player but Geoff Lawson worked out that a leg slip could be his downfall.
(Patrick Eagar/Getty Images)

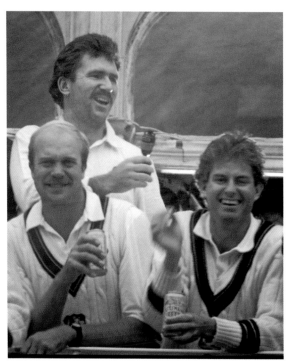

It's hard to see us for the champagne in the air, but Carl Rackemann, Terry and I are celebrating regaining the Ashes 4–0 on the balcony at The Oval. It was a good day.
(Patrick Eagar/Getty Images)

In 1990–91 we retained the Ashes when England next came out to Australia, winning 3–0. Mark Waugh scored a century on debut and became a valuable part of our team and the slips cordon. (David Munden/ Popperfoto/Getty Images)

We went into the 1992 World Cup, held in Sydney, as favourites, but unfortunately were knocked out in the group rounds. Pakistan went on to win, under Imran Khan, beating England. It was South Africa's first World Cup after the apartheid suspensions. (Adrian Murrell/Getty Images)

appreciate the power-hitting and the fact that those skills have flowed through to the 50-over game. Who would have thought you could make 350 and lose, but that's what's now happening at 50-over level. The guys are fitter, they have no inhibitions, they're stronger athletes and it's resulted in these incredible scores.

Twenty20 cricket is a bit of a lottery, with a smaller sample of overs, and therefore unpredictable. That's probably one reason it's so popular—almost anyone can win. It's like me playing Tiger Woods in golf. If I played him in a one-hole competition at Brookwater tomorrow I could beat him, but I'd never beat him over 18 holes, and a four-round golf tournament equates to a Test match in cricket. In Test cricket, there's generally a chance to pull yourself back into a game after a rough patch. But in Twenty20, if you drop off the pace, you're usually finished.

The message is that you have to dominate, you can't let the game drift, you have to get after the bowling. Back when I played 50-over cricket, if someone had said, 'We'll give you 225 and you don't have to bat,' we'd just about have taken that, although it sounds ridiculous now. In the eighties at the MCG, for instance, you'd accept that total because it's such a big ground, the tactics were different and the equipment was inferior to the modern gear.

The mentality of the players is also different. Their expectation is that you'll go at five, six, up to 10 runs per over. A guy like David Warner is interesting, because his style of play is 'see it, hit it', but now he's realising the benefit of his improved technique and patience. Nevertheless, he still goes at almost a run a ball, even in Test cricket. I think there'll be a flow-on to Test cricket, and the scoring rates will be quicker, but I do look at techniques as well and it worries me a little. I'm not sure the plethora of short-form cricket has helped the techniques of players for Test cricket, because they all want to play everything, and to play Twenty20 cricket they need that power game. Some of these guys may struggle if they're stuck in on a green wicket in a Test match, but then again, most people do.

The bats are huge, but I don't see any problem with that. I bought a bat for my son Lachlan just recently—a Spartan, which is basically the same as Michael Clarke's bat—and it's a huge piece of wood. I put it up against one of my old Duncan Fearnley bats and the difference is amazing. But that doesn't bother me, because there are other factors involved. You have a fitter, stronger athlete and better equipment, plus the boundaries are in. I used to have to hit the ball at 95 per cent of my power and timing to hit a six; now they have to hit it at about 70 per cent.

In Twenty20 cricket, the pitches favour batting and they don't change too much. I don't think the adjustments are as significant for that game, and your technique isn't tested so much. But the power-hitting is sensational, and you only have to watch someone like Glenn Maxwell flogging the ball all over the park to realise how powerful the players have become. In a Twenty20 match in India, his team, Kings XI Punjab, made 238 in their 20 overs, and 160 from the last ten overs! We used to knock up 250 at the MCG in a 50-over game and that was a winning score. I'm sure the bowlers will fight back, but it's getting harder, because the Twenty20 game isn't designed for bowlers.

I take my hat off to the modern player, I really do. They've taken the game to another level. You just have to watch old footage of the game we played. I think players of my era could fit into the current era quite easily in terms of Test cricket, but could we go into a Twenty20 game? No, not as we were. We'd have to improve and we'd have to change.

SWITCH-HITTING HAS become popular in the Twenty20 game, mainly through reverse sweeping but in a few cases through actually changing hands midstream. David Warner gave a brilliant illustration of this in a Twenty20 international between Australia and India at the WACA Ground in 2012. He faced up in his usual left-handed way against the spinner Ravi Ashwin, then changed his grip and switched to right-handed as Ashwin bowled, and dispatched the ball into the crowd. Kevin Pietersen of England is another highly gifted player who has managed that particular shot, switching from right-handed to left-handed.

It's typical of the kind of innovation Twenty20 cricket has brought to the modern game, although there's also been debate about whether switching hands, as Warner and Pietersen have done, ought to be outlawed. Of course the usual reverse sweeping, where you slap the ball away but don't change your grip, is fine. But, much as I hate to stifle innovation, I believe the Warner shot should be outlawed. It's not fair to the bowler, that shot, even if it's incredibly skilful. My gut feeling is that the bowler and his captain have set a field for a batsman who's, say, right-handed. You wouldn't allow a bowler to run up then suddenly sneak across and bowl around the wicket, because the laws say you must inform the batsman, and a bowler can't change from, say, right-arm to left-arm deliveries as he runs in. Fair has to be fair.

THE BOWLERS WILL always find a way, though. Many people think Twenty20 cricket is the death of the bowler, and I have a lot of conversations with bowlers who complain about the domination of the bat. But I always say, 'The game isn't designed like that. Good bowlers will always find a way to be in the game.' That's why great bowlers are like gold nuggets. They win you matches.

There's been a massive change in modern cricket, for instance, since bowlers have been allowed up to 15 degrees of flex in the arm. We're seeing the so-called doosra and spinners delivering balls that go the other way. I doubt you could do that legally under the old rules, but with the

15-degree limit introduced by the ICC you can. The common theme is that 'People don't turn up to see someone bowl', but they actually do. People like watching great bowlers like Shane Warne and Dennis Lillee, because they're a cut above the others and they'll take their teams to victories.

But people like to see good-quality batting as well. In Twenty20 cricket you don't want a 50 to 49 scoreline; you want 150 to 149. So I wouldn't take the big bats away. The bowlers will develop their skills; they'll bowl yorkers and slower balls and new types of deliveries, and the spinners will still play a role. We just saw in the 2014 Twenty20 World Cup in Bangladesh that of the top ten spots for bowlers, nine were for spinners. People thought these shorter games would be the death of the spinner, but in fact the opposite is the case.

I think the popularity of Twenty20 will flow on to other forms of the game, which can only be good. The kids want to play shorter forms of cricket and the family will follow them along, and then maybe the mums and dads will move their interest to longer-form cricket. Don't forget, we've got a lot of immigrants in this country from parts of the world where cricket is non-existent, so are those people going to sit there and watch a game for five days? Who are we kidding? But they might convert to one-day cricket, a 50-over game, because they like watching David Warner bat, and then go along to watch a Test match to see him bat, or watch him on television after that.

I also like the new shots and the innovative ways the current generation play. The ramp shot, for instance, or the reverse sweep, which is a fantastic weapon. A captain blocks off one side of the field, so you swap over and hit it to the vacant side, as Glenn Maxwell or David Warner do. That shot barely existed when I played, and on the one occasion I tried it, I ended up getting hit in the mouth! If I played now, I'd have to learn those types of shots.

The bowlers are bound to innovate as well, using their slower balls. Think how productive Simon O'Donnell and Steve Waugh were in the eighties with that slow ball that came from the back of the hand—it hoodwinked a lot of players back then. Nowadays the players are developing a lot of new balls, and maybe it's come to the point where we've forgotten how to bowl a good yorker. That's the best ball in short-form cricket, and that's never changed. Why not bowl it every time? Maybe because the modern Twenty20 player has developed the ramp shot to counter-act it, but it's still a very hard ball to score off.

Guys now are getting hundreds in less than 50 balls in Twenty20 cricket, which is just incredible. It used to be that if you got a side to the point where they needed six runs an over, a run per ball, you were at break-even point, and if you pushed them past that the odds were stacked in your favour. In modern cricket, if a team needs 10 runs an over, that's fine by them. They're happy to let it swell out to ten, and the breaking point is probably around 12 runs an over. But even then it's not safe!

In 2013, Royal Challengers Bangalore scored 5–263 in a Twenty20 game during the IPL competition, a world record. Individually, Chris Gayle's 175 not out from 66 balls in the same game for Bangalore is the high-water mark. Gayle is perfect for Twenty20 cricket: power *and* technique! He hit 17 sixes in that innings and reached his hundred in 30 balls. Yuvraj Singh of India has made 50 in 12 balls. It's ridiculously quick scoring.

I think the game has moved on well, and I'm certainly not one of those people who reckons cricket was better in my day. The game has evolved and become far more professional. The players are fitter, stronger and better prepared because they're full-time, so it would be blinkered to think the game hasn't developed. It's ridiculous to think that anything else could be the case.

THE BIG BASH is great, but I do think it goes for too long and should be condensed. You could have double-headers—one in the afternoon and one in the evening—so that it runs over four weeks instead of six.

I don't mind the franchise-type model, where the players take the opportunities as they arise. Most of the franchises will try to hang on to four or five core players, then it's just a matter of seeing which players on the market will fit into what you're trying to do as a team, all under a salary cap of $1.2 million. It would be wonderful if the Aussie internationals, such as David Warner, could play half the games, but at the moment they're not always released. I know it's difficult in the middle of a Test series to swap from one form to another, but if we're serious about developing the Big Bash, we have to encourage and allow the top players to play.

As I SAID, the money is amazing. Guys like Chris Gayle and Glenn Maxwell could go and play anywhere; they don't really need to play for their countries. They can go and play in the Caribbean Twenty20 league, the Sri Lankan league, in England, the Big Bash here, and earn several million dollars a year. But I do think Maxwell will end up playing Test cricket. He'll present a compelling argument to the selectors: he bowls some spin, he fields brilliantly, but has he got technique? I think he has.

The money has been part of the evolution of the game, and I'm not going to complain. I think I was lucky being a post-WSC player; there's no doubt the pay increased as a result. The interesting question would be what the percentages were back then. At the moment the players get 26 per cent of Cricket Australia's earnings. Would we have got 26 per cent of the pie? No way of knowing, and the pie was a lot smaller then.

The Twenty20 revolution

Australian cricket is turning over more than $200 million per annum and the players are getting 26 per cent of that, which is more than $50 million, split between the state-contracted players and the internationals. The guys on the top contracts have to be on $1.5–2 million, and if you throw in $1 million for IPL, your endorsements, your bat contracts, a top-ranked player would be up around $5 million. That's a seriously good earn. India has become such a lucrative market for cricketers. When Australia plays India in a 50-over international, Cricket Australia makes something like $7 million.

Towards the end of my career it probably reached a point where we were being underpaid for what the game was generating, and as a result, the players formed the Australian Cricketers' Association and payments spiked. Throw in India's rise, the television rights and the Twenty20 revolution, and the players' potential earnings have gone through the roof. If the players are getting 26 per cent, that means there's 74 per cent left to run the game, and that's a pretty good formula. Everyone says, 'The players are paid too much,' but they're just getting their slice of the pie, even if it's really good money by normal standards.

I know people say, 'The more you get, the more you want,' but the players can set themselves up for the future, and it's a different mindset from my day. We talked about lots of different things, but never share portfolios or the latest BMW. That's just the progression of the sport, but it's a good thing, because in this country you have AFL, rugby league, rugby union and soccer all trying to attract the best athletes. Cricket can now put a serious, compelling argument to a multi-talented youngster: 'You follow our game, you can play till your mid-thirties or older, the stresses on your body will be lower than for running around on a football field, and you can earn a seriously good income.' Players are spat out pretty quickly from the football codes. All professional sport is the same, but at least cricket is competing financially.

WHAT HAPPENS TO 50-over cricket in this environment, now that Twenty20 is so popular? A few people believe the 20-over form has basically filled the slot previously taken by 50-over cricket but I'm not so sure about that. I think the 50-over game, with its powerplays and further fielding restrictions, is a superior game to Twenty20 cricket, because you can get yourself into strife but still have time to get yourself out again. There are different phases of that game, and I prefer it as a contest between bat and ball.

In saying all this, I think we're playing a bit too much 50-over cricket, but that will continue for as long as it keeps making money. For me, less is more, and a five-match series could be cut back to a three-match series. There were times when we were playing up to eight one-dayers in a series, which was fantastic financially, but is it ideal in the long run? I think 50-over cricket still has a huge role to play in the international sphere, especially if it's refined into more meaningful series with fewer matches, followed by a World Cup every four years. As far as Twenty20 cricket is concerned, I'd keep the World Cup, played every two years, but I wouldn't play many Twenty20 internationals apart from that. I'd keep Twenty20 a predominantly domestic game.

4

The modern game

FALLING CROWDS AT Test matches are a worry for international cricket, at least outside of Australia and England, where the numbers are still quite strong. Most likely we promote it better, or perhaps our cricket communities have a better mindset and are happy to go along and watch Test cricket, even when we don't play each other. But around the globe it's quite staggering. To think that South Africa was the No. 1 country in Test cricket but couldn't even draw big crowds for the series against Australia this year to decide which was world champion! On Boxing Day 2013, Australia played England before a world record 91,092 at the MCG, the highest single-day crowd for a Test match in the 130-odd year history of Tests. On the same day at Durban,

South Africa played India before just 13,000 people. Something is wrong.

We promote Test cricket as the pinnacle of the game, and I think England are the same. We put money into it, and the baggy green cap is a huge honour. The 50-over and Twenty20 caps are a huge achievement, but the Australian players really want the baggy green cap. For the true believers, the baggy green is what it's all about and the players are very mindful of it—that makes me, for one, extremely happy.

But Test cricket needs to get its act together in certain areas. The game needs to keep ticking over, and there are far too many breaks for drinks, injury treatment and wicket referrals to the third umpire. We used to have to bowl a minimum of 90 overs in six hours; now it's 90 overs in six and a half hours and the players still struggle to manage that.

I know there's a duty-of-care issue with injuries, but the constant delays frustrate me. If a batsman is badly hurt, that's unfortunate, but he should have to get off the ground. I hate it when a batsman is hit and there's a ten-minute delay while he gets some kind of magic spray applied by the physiotherapist or, just as time-consumingly, changes his helmet. It shouldn't take that long. If you're badly hurt, get off; if not, play on.

Then there are all the drinks that come onto the ground for players. Look, I'm all for hydration. I know we almost killed Dean Jones in the tied Test at Chennai in 1986 because of dehydration, so I have to be all for it. But it's not that difficult for players to get a drink without holding up the game. Nowadays, there need only be an appeal by the fielding side followed by a decision review, and both sides have their back-up guys out on the field with drinks. Then the decision comes down as 'not out', and we've wasted a few minutes. Of course, they should be ready to bowl the next ball if the decision is in the negative. That should only take ten seconds, but invariably it's a minute or two. Then there's another appeal two balls later, a review is asked for and more drinks come onto the field. I don't think my bladder could take it! When you add up all these delays, there's too much time wastage in Test cricket.

This should be policed properly. If a team can do all that and still bowl 90 overs or more in six hours, that's fine by me. But if they can't, it's an issue. In Twenty20 cricket they nearly always bowl their overs on time because it's strictly policed. Why not police it more diligently in Test cricket?

STOPPAGES FOR BAD light in Test cricket drive me mad. Like most sports, cricket is fundamentally dangerous and there's an element of risk to players. In other words, you can get hit in the head at midday and be seriously hurt. If you get hurt at 5.55 pm in murky light, people might say it's too dark, but the injury hasn't happened because the player can't see the ball. I was offered the chance to go off for bad light maybe ten times in my career, and I can put my hand on my heart and say as a batsman that I never came off because I couldn't see the ball. The fielders might say it's tough to see, but you have to look at game scenarios.

If you're smashing the opposition all over the place and trying to set a target for a declaration, you won't come off for bad light; you'll stay to score as many runs as you can. In these cases it's the bowling side saying they can't see the ball. But have you ever seen a team come off when they're two-down and they have 20 runs to get? It's 5.55 pm and getting dark, but they'll stay out there till midnight if they have to. That makes a joke of the rule as it stands. Is it the fear of litigation, the worry of being sued by an injured player for failing to take care of the athletes? I played a hell of a lot of cricket, and I can say that in 99 per cent of cases the light rules are used as a tactic to get off the ground at the end of a day's play so that the batting team can preserve wickets.

It brings to mind a 50-over game I played in many years ago at the WACA in Perth. Australia were playing the West Indies and it was a day game starting at 10 am. We batted first and I went to the crease in the first over of the match on a hat-trick. It was the fastest and scariest bowling I ever faced. Michael Holding was steaming in from the Lillee Marsh Stand end of the ground with a white ball. The sun was shining but was still low in the sky, and the pitch in those days was rock hard, with a sheen to the surface. With the pace and bounce Michael was getting, plus the difficulty picking up the white ball in those conditions, it's the most scared I've ever been out in the middle. My point is that it was dangerous, and the light was such that picking up the ball was extremely difficult, so why didn't the umpires come off the ground? What's the difference between that scenario and murky light at 5.55 pm?

Nowadays, the umpires are in control and they use light meters out in the middle, but they're too conservative in the way they handle bad light. They'll say, 'In our opinion it's too hard to see the ball,' and they have the final say. The old laws, which gave umpires the right to 'offer' bad light to the batsmen, were removed in 2010. Here's what the current laws say:

Law 3.8 Fitness for play

(a) It is solely for the umpires together to decide whether either conditions of ground, weather or light or exceptional circumstances mean that it would be dangerous or unreasonable for play to take place.

Law 3.9 Suspension of play in dangerous or unreasonable conditions

b) If at any time the umpires together agree that the conditions of ground, weather or light, or any other circumstances are dangerous or unreasonable, they shall immediately suspend play, or not allow play to start or to recommence.

The key word there is 'dangerous'. The English umpire Dickie Bird once said that the only way to be fair and consistent about bad-light interruptions was to play until it was virtually dark, meaning it literally. I agree with him. In modern cricket the umpires use their light meters, take a reading, and that becomes the standard for the whole match, so that every time the light deteriorates to that point over the next few days, they're obliged to take the players off. It could be with a side two-down and 10 runs to win. If I was the bowling side, I'd be saying, 'I want the light checked.' It's a ridiculous situation that we have to tighten up. It has to be a lot more difficult to come off, particularly in an environment where it's hard enough to draw spectators to the game. Cricket's dangerous at any time. That's part of the deal.

NIGHT TEST MATCHES interest me. I played Sheffield Shield cricket for Queensland at night in the nineties when Cricket Australia experimented with an orange ball and a yellow ball for a few games, and I enjoyed them immensely. Sadly, the notion died off at the time, not so much through lack of interest as through the realisation that the Sheffield Shield competition is there to develop Test players, and at that time there was very little chance of playing day–night Test cricket, so what was the point? But Cricket Australia had some more night Shield games in the 2013–14 season with a pink ball, and they intend playing some Test cricket under lights quite soon. The series against New Zealand in 2015–16 has been mentioned as a possibility, subject to the approval of all concerned. James Sutherland, the Cricket Australia chief executive, believes it's worth trying: 'It's about securing the future relevance of Test cricket as a sport of choice not just here but all around the world,' he said recently.

The ball is an issue, and a lot of people don't realise that the red ball is impregnated with dye while the white ball we use for Twenty20 and 50-over cricket is painted. The white ball scuffs up and will only last around 25 overs or so before it turns grey and becomes difficult to see, while the red ball is too dark to be used at night. So a pink ball might end up being the answer.

It's a great idea in theory, but in practice you can probably only play in Australia and England because of conditions. In South Africa, Pakistan and India you often get a very heavy dew at night, which makes the ball hard to handle for bowlers and fieldsmen. The use of spin becomes very difficult under these conditions. For one-day cricket, the players just put up with it, and in the Twenty20 World Cup in Bangladesh this year, the games were affected by it, particularly later in the evening. In the shorter form of the game, the ball itself is of little importance compared to the longer form, where the maintenance and shining of the ball is vital to the tactics. So, I'm not sure where we're going to play these night Tests. If they're only played in Australia, for instance, that would give us a huge advantage because we'll be playing Shield cricket at night. In the English summer it doesn't get dark until 9–10 pm, so you might only have an hour when the lights are in full use. Overall, you want the game to be as close to normal, tactical cricket as possible. I'm certainly in favour of trying it.

I'd also consider breaking Test cricket into two pools, with promotion and relegation every two years. You'd accumulate points and there'd be a top six and a bottom six taken from the world rankings. There'd be some very interesting Test matches played under that system, and it would also give each game extra relevance. I'd like to see Ireland and the Netherlands playing, since they showed something in the Twenty20 World Cup. It's definitely an idea for the authorities to ponder.

Is there too much cricket? I don't believe so. Maybe just a little tinkering is required with the amount of one-day cricket played. To generate the income through television rights, you just have to play the days. The players know the money comes from television rights—that there might be 100 days of cricket to play and they'll get paid x dollars to complete that assignment and earn the income. They're pragmatic. The players are on a pretty good wicket, and they know it.

The modern game

I wouldn't use any sort of formal rotation system for players, such as the one that was in place during recent times in Australia. I'd play my best sides as often as possible, which Darren Lehmann is doing as the current Australian coach. What you do need, though, is a more *natural* rotation system, a more intuitive system with more emphasis on common sense, taking into account that it's very difficult for players to play every single game.

The rotation system of recent years was very unpopular with the public, and to me it gave too much credence to the sports scientists monitoring the workloads of the players, and in particular the fast bowlers. I'd do it more intuitively: 'Your pace is down, you look a bit jaded to me. Have the next game off.' The slightly ridiculous thing about the previous system was that you might rotate guys out of internationals every summer, yet those same guys would go and play eight weeks of Twenty20 cricket in India. I'd do the same for a million dollars! But how do you justify leaving that player out of a one-day game in Australia to give him a rest from excessive workload? You can't. I'd argue that if he's fit, and in form, he's playing.

If a fast bowler said to me, 'I feel great. I'm in form,' I wouldn't rotate him. I'd trust him to give an honest assessment of his health, and I think Darren Lehmann has done that. We were rotating people out of games for no reason other than rotation. I understand that the statistics show that if you're under 25 you're probably going to get an injury, but let's play them and, if they get injured, fix them. Why try to predict an injury that might never happen? The scientists can't tell me, 'He'll break down if he bowls another ball.' They can't be so sure.

I have a theory—and I'll admit it isn't based on anything more than my own observations—that fast bowlers go better when they keep their engine ticking over. They're like old taxis. They do hundreds of thousands of kilometres; they're always churning away, with the engine running and the oil pumping through the system. They end up running a lot longer than a normal city car that's continually stopping and starting.

I don't think fast bowlers actually bowl enough. I'm not saying they should bowl *every* day, but certainly *most* days. Net sessions are about keeping the engine ticking over, teaching your body what you want it to do, and it doesn't have to be done at 100 per cent intensity, and therefore you build up the muscles in the right areas. I look at the West Indies in the eighties, I look at Sir Richard Hadlee and I look at Glenn McGrath, who just kept turning over. McGrath always thought he was more vulnerable to injury when he'd stopped for a while and then came back from a break.

All those West Indian greats from the eighties played county cricket and they played international cricket, bowling enormous numbers of overs. Courtney Walsh was another advocate for keeping the engine going; he might not always have gone flat chat, but he just kept ticking over. He's one of only four bowlers to have delivered more than 5000 overs in Test cricket, the other three (Muttiah Muralitharan, Shane Warne and Anil Kumble) all being spinners. Walsh bowled 30,000 balls in Test cricket, more than 10,000 in one-day cricket and 85,000 in first-class cricket. He rarely broke down, just like an old taxi.

I understand the fears about the skeletal frame and how it takes time for a young bowler's body to develop and harden. Many of them, such as Patrick Cummins and James Pattinson, have broken down; even Dennis Lillee was a young tearaway who broke down with a back stress fracture, then tightened his action and returned. Maybe it's inevitable for young fast bowlers to be injured. But you can't keep them from bowling until they're 25!

CRICKET NEEDS TO track the kids who come to the game early but are then lost to other sports, particularly AFL. If a lad is spat out of the football system at 23, if at all possible he should be drawn back to cricket, assuming he played the game at a reasonable level in his early years. Many of them are talented cricketers. We should be saying, 'Have a crack at the AFL or the NRL by all means, but if it doesn't work out, come back and we'll fast-track you, because we know you had great potential at 17.'

In cricket, we have 18 top-level contracts plus the Sheffield Shield contracts, so around 140 contracts at any given time, plus rookies. The top Shield contracts are better than $100,000 now, and there's been a logjam of players because they're staying in the game longer. A cricket career nowadays is between the ages of about 25 and 35, when it used to be between 20 and 30. It just takes longer for most young players to get into their teams at state level. So my point is, if I'm an AFL player and the system spits me out at 23, that gives me two years or so to get back into my cricket before I'm likely even to be looked at. Why not give it a crack?

This is the problem for cricket, filling the gap between kids coming out of the under-19 system and actually cracking it in the big time. That's where state associations must be proactive. If you have a guy in his thirties who's not going to play for Australia and he's not necessarily filling a leadership role, he might be a journeyman and a good cricketer, but he might have to be moved on. The state associations need to encourage youth and make some hard decisions. This isn't an easy situation, because cricket is now a career, and if performances are still good then the question is: 'Why retire?'

CRICKET'S DECISION REVIEW system (DRS) has its good points. Of course, the use of television replays has been brilliant in making line decisions—on run-outs and stumpings, for instance. It's a definitive situation and I applaud that. But the natural progression was to take video replays further, and that's where we've hit some difficulties in the game. The technologies were developed for television and its viewers, not necessarily to rule on decisions.

I've watched it unfold and I've also watched the system in place in the NRL, and I'm not sure whether it's actually better than the old way. Every weekend there's a drama in the NRL with decision reviews. Was it a shepherd? Was it a forward pass? Was it a try? They have the option of reviewing virtually every part of the game, but is this a good or a bad thing? I note that in baseball they tried a review system in 2008 for home-run calls, and quickly tossed it. More recently, baseball has allowed one challenge per team with a review system, but they've been very conservative in the way they've brought in the change. Sometimes the introduction of technology causes more problems than it set out to resolve.

It seems to me that cricketers are using decision reviews as a tactic rather than really believing the umpire has made a mistake. 'We've got two reviews left and Michael Clarke's batting. Did he nick it down the leg side? We're really not sure, but let's give it a go because we have the reviews there.' That's the thinking and it's not surprising. When I was in India for the 2013 series Australia lost, the Indians wouldn't allow the DRS for anything other than line appeals, and it wasn't that bad. There were times when you'd watch and think, 'I wouldn't mind a review of that,' but if there's not that option the players just get on with it.

The issue is that the technology isn't perfect and can't be fully trusted. I've seen quite a few examples where the Hawk-Eye system—which simulates the flight of the ball—shows the ball hitting the stumps but the actual television replay shows the ball missing! Then you have the ball-half-in or ball-half-out situation, which just causes more confusion. With Hot Spot for nicks, there are times when it doesn't show up a little feather nick from the bat. And we're using the Snicko system ahead of an umpire's opinion, but it might only indicate that you snicked your pad or even have a creaky bat handle. With my traditionalist's hat on, I'd argue that we should leave the technology out of it other than for line decisions.

Having said that, I understand that the DRS will stay in some form. The idea is to get rid of the howler decision, the horrendous error by an umpire. I'd suggest, as a starter, cutting the number of reviews to one per team. That way, teams would have to be almost 100 per cent sure that a mistake has been made before they launch a review. At the moment, they're too speculative—how many times have we seen a player get it completely wrong when he asks for a review? Maybe we should just hand the review system back to the umpires. Mind you, then every appeal would be checked, just in case!

•

The modern game

ONE THING ABOUT DRS that annoys me is the no-ball check after a wicket falls. Often now when a wicket is taken, the umpire will ask the third umpire to review if the bowler overstepped, which is totally unnecessary and has the effect of making a good moment anticlimactic.

I'd ask the host broadcaster not to show no-ball replays at all. I'd go to, say, David Gyngell, the head of Channel Nine, and say, 'Look, we have a problem with you showing replays of no-balls after wickets. It's not a big part of the game, and if the umpire misses it by a millimetre, so be it.' So you don't even show the no-balls on television. It would also work for the broadcasters, because no one wants the game extending beyond the very expensive satellite time they're budgeted for, or interfering with regular shows. It's just not necessary to police the no-balls any more than the umpires do already by watching where the bowlers' feet land, and if you don't know as a viewer, you're none the wiser. No-balls are just not a big part of the game.

It's incredibly difficult for umpires, because they're trying to pick up no-balls and then focus on the striker's end for lbw, caught behind and all the other dismissals. The bowler's heel tends to slide, and they have so many other things to concern themselves with. I know that my mate Dean Jones is an advocate for the controlling umpire focusing only on the striker's end and not looking for no-balls at all. With his total concentration on the batsman facing, I believe we'd get better decisions. What it would require, of course, is that someone else police the no-balls because you can't have the bowler overstepping by huge margins and getting away with it.

One option would be to leave run-outs totally to the third umpire, because inevitably, if it's close, the umpires will refer them anyway. They don't pretend their eyes are better than a television camera that's exactly side-on. That second umpire could stand somewhere at the other end, near the stumps, and police the no-balls. Either that, or you leave the no-ball calls to the third umpire. I know this could be unwieldy, but I truly believe you'd get a better result.

THE SCRUTINY ON umpires today is very harsh, and overall I believe they're better than they used to be, despite one or two controversies. I do like the neutrality that was introduced for Test matches by the ICC when it instigated a central panel of the best umpires. It removed that perception that was prevalent in my playing days that teams could be dudded by hometown umpiring. It took that question mark away.

The only point I dislike about the central panel is that an umpire can't officiate in a Test match in his own country. It must have been frustrating for Simon Taufel, who was the No. 1 umpire in the world for years yet could never enjoy the thrill of standing in a Test in Australia. But the central panel removes the conspiracy theories that did the rounds in my day. The late Tony Greig used to wind us up by saying, 'Bill Lawry was never given out lbw in Australia!'

I don't like batsmen being told to stop and wait for reviews, or no-ball rulings from the third umpire. As a player, you're educated to cop decisions on the chin. You get good and bad decisions, and there are swings and roundabouts, as they say. Of course, it's difficult to cop a bad one, even if it's part of the game, but you just have to.

In England in 2013 we had Stuart Broad's infamous non-dismissal, when he was taken cleanly at slip by Michael Clarke off Ashton Agar's spin but given not out by umpire Aleem Dar. In that case, Australia had already used its two referrals for the innings, so that really obvious one slipped through. Broad nicked the ball to slip but umpire Dar apparently thought it had also clipped the glove of wicket-keeper Brad Haddin and that this had caused the deviation rather than a nick. In that instance, the Australians were at fault for wasting both their reviews. That's one reason I'd like to see the number of referrals cut to one, so that teams are surer of themselves before asking.

The DRS is here to stay, though. I saw a statistic recently that umpires were getting 92 per cent of decisions correct before the DRS was broadened, and now it's gone up to 95 per cent. Will we ever get 100 per cent? I think not.

INDIA'S POWER IN world cricket causes a lot of comment in Australia, but it's just a reality and it's been the case for a long time, even before the explosion of the IPL and the money it brought into the game. India produces around 80 per cent of the game's revenue, so why shouldn't it have a big say in how that business is run? India flourishes in cricket because Australia and England in particular play biennial cricket matches, television rights have exploded, and they've happened upon the IPL money-spinner. But without England and Australia, India would lose a lot of television-rights cash, and the IPL wouldn't be the same if it only included Indian players. The Indians depend on homegrown stars, but they also need the overseas stars.

We're not blameless, because Australia and England did the same thing for years in cricket. Everyone just needs to take a deep breath and say, 'Look, we all flourish if we work together.' Recently we signed a pact with England and India, which basically means we've taken over the ICC and taken more of a say in the split of revenue. Previously, the ten main countries were getting equal shares, but did Zimbabwe deserve that share, or Bangladesh? I guess they'd argue that for the development of the game, they need that share. But the ICC isn't like FIFA, football's ruling body. It's not all-controlling.

The big countries do their own thing most of the time anyway. India doesn't even bother adhering to the Future Tours Programme the ICC put together; they tend not to play Bangladesh, for instance, because it costs them too much money—it's simpler and cheaper to pay the fine. The ICC introduced referees and the umpiring panel, but on the big-ticket items like the finances, the reality is that India get what they want.

5

Batting

MICHAEL CLARKE COULD be one of our greatest players. He's blossomed so much in recent years, especially since he became Australia's captain, and while we overuse the term *great*, he belongs in that category. He has 8000 runs at a 50-plus average; he's made a triple hundred and double hundreds. That innings he played in South Africa in 2014, when he was battered around at Newlands by Morné Morkel, was typical of his development. Clarke was out of touch—had only made 60 runs in the first two Tests of that series—and Morkel, who's quick and bouncy, stuck it to him with the short stuff. A lot of people think Michael is a little soft, being a sensitive type of guy, the modern cricketer, but he actually has plenty of ticker. On that day in South Africa he extracted 161 not out; Morkel didn't get a wicket, let alone Michael's; and Australia won. It's as well as Clarke has played anywhere.

The responsibilities of being captain don't seem to bother him. In fact, I'd guess that it's heightened his awareness of those burdens and improved his focus. He's always had the talent, but he's grown in recent times. He plays all the shots; he doesn't have an obvious weakness, other than possibly against a good short ball, early in his innings. He's also a great player of spin. Against England at the Gabba last season he looked to be in trouble against the short ball in the first innings. Then he came back in the second dig and played a blinder, got 148 and took every bit of short-pitched stuff Jimmy Anderson, Stuart Broad and Chris Tremlett could send his way. Australia won again.

If Michael's dodgy back holds up, I suspect he'll overtake Ricky Ponting (13,378) and me (11,174) to become Australia's highest Test run-scorer. At the time of writing he's fifth on the Australian list at 8240 runs, with Ponting, me, Steve Waugh (10,927) and Matthew Hayden (8625) ahead of him. But at 33 he's playing as well as ever, so I see no reason why he shouldn't go right to the top of that list. The record will back up what we see. He's also an outstanding one-day cricketer, which of course is a big part of the equation in the modern era. He can be an iconic player and he can go as far as he wants.

•

Batting

I WAS A huge Ricky Ponting fan. The game never drifted when he was at the crease. He went in early and often under the pump as the first-drop man, but he'd counter-attack in that situation, and he was very difficult to bowl to. With his love of the pull shot and his wonderful driving, the degree of error for the bowler would be about a metre at most. Too short, and he'd cut or pull, too full and he'd drive. And he had no fear with his execution of shots. Was he better than Greg Chappell? Well, you can debate that. Actually, I think that for most people Greg is out of sight, out of mind, given his time was longer ago, and people tend to forget exactly how good he was. Ponting and Greg Chappell are my two best Aussies at the moment, but you could throw Steve Waugh in there, too, and Michael Clarke is running up to that group quite quickly.

Steve Waugh took three years to get a hundred in a Test match, a full 27 matches, which was a sketchy start. He was identified as a player of the future and he held his place in the side through his one-day cricket more than his Test form. He ebbed and flowed in Test cricket before he cemented it on the 1989 Ashes tour, which was a watershed tour for him. Even then, Steve was dropped a couple of years later, so he had to work hard to establish himself more than once.

IN RECENT TIMES, David Warner has improved his all-round game, Chris Rogers has been excellent, and Shane Watson makes up the engine room of the current team. Shane Watson is one of my favourite players to watch. But I find Shane frustrating as a batsman, and his record says that he's a good player but not the great player he should be! Shane averages 36.25 in Tests, which tells you that, but he's such a talent when he's on song.

Watson has a forward press that at times bothers me. It's a technical thing—his left foot goes to the same spot every time, and then he plays around his front leg. Most batsmen have a trigger that activates their feet when a bowler delivers, particularly a quick bowler. Personally, I used to duck my head a little bit and shuffle across. I tried to keep myself from ducking too much over the years, but if I was out of form it became worse. When Greg Chappell used to say, 'You're bobbing your head,' I knew I'd have to work at cutting it down. It was ingrained as my 'get ready' trigger, and Brian Lara did it a little as well. Some batsmen, like Mark Waugh and Matthew Hayden, stay quite still, but most will have a little movement at the instant the bowler releases the ball.

I'm not saying Watson's forward press is necessarily a bad thing; it's obviously his trigger movement. I don't believe there's just one method of batting that's gospel, but the way he plants his foot is causing him some grief; he needs somewhere to go from there, another move. You can't just plant and play every shot from that spot.

Batting

I'm not sure whether 'Watto' needs to open his stance more, or focus on a back press or more of a shuffle. I'm not a batting coach per se, but I'm sure it's costing him a lot of runs. He's good enough to average in the forties in Test cricket, so it's frustrating that he's below that.

The team has had trouble finding his best position, too. Probably over the journey he's played best as an opener, but Chris Rogers and David Warner seem to be settled at the top, so he's picked up the all-important No. 3 spot, where we're still questionable. Then there's his bowling, which is actually very good. Should we be using him as a No. 6 so that he can bowl a bit? That would make the team balance perfect.

STEVE SMITH HAS emerged as a cracking batsman for Australia. Players have been in and out of the side over the last couple of years because we were losing a bit, but the selectors still made some conscious choices: 'This guy is good, some of these guys are dominating Sheffield Shield cricket, so we've got to pick and stick.' Steve's one of those who's been identified, and he's a smart kid. He's started to work his game out. He feels more comfortable with what works for him and what doesn't in the Test environment. He's become a very important player, with four centuries and an average of 40.02. That's quite a good return in his first 20 Tests, and I'm convinced it will get better.

Steve's playing style was a bit loose at the start, but he's tightened up in recent times.

The natural evolution for him is to keep improving with his batting but then bowl some leg-spinners, which he does well. He also has the potential to captain the Australian team. He was pushed up to the captaincy of New South Wales and they won the Sheffield Shield under his leadership, so he'd be a good choice. His youth is also in his favour, because traditionally with Australian captains, we look for some longevity. We tend not to pick a captain who's in danger of only being around for five minutes. The other alternative as a future captain would be David Warner, who has a good cricket brain and is a feisty competitor, but I'd like to see him play some more cricket before he's considered as captain. It will all depend on how long Michael Clarke can stay fit and keen and playing well. I know Michael has talked about not lingering for too long, not playing until he's 40 or so, but I believe he'll be around for a while yet, and I imagine that while he's there he'll retain the captaincy.

PHIL HUGHES HAS already been dropped twice, casting some doubts on his ability to play at the top level, but I don't share the scepticism about his batting. I like him, not so much because he's pretty to watch, but for a simpler reason: he scores big runs. His technique isn't perfect, but at the time of writing he's scored 26 first-class hundreds and three Test tons as well as two one-day international hundreds for Australia. He accumulates runs wherever he plays, and this is a very nice habit for a batsman to adopt.

I believe that when Hughes was dropped in England in 2009, after a few problems against the English fast bowlers, it was a premature decision. He'd made runs in South Africa in the same year, and while he was out of sorts in England, he had a few mates. But Hughes could end up being like Justin Langer, who had to wait a long time to cement a place in the Test team. Hughes is 25 years old, and the truth is that most guys will hit a rocky patch when they reach the international level but the good ones will come back. Getting dropped isn't a problem in itself, it's more of a challenge. Look at Steve Waugh, who was dropped more than once, and Matthew Hayden. There's no disgrace in it.

Phil has a good attitude; he likes to fight. Technically, he can occasionally close himself off, moving his back foot towards leg stump, which made him deadly when bowlers pushed the ball wide of off stump—before they worked out that they needed to bowl *at* him. More recently, he's worked on moving towards a back-and-across movement, so that he's in a far better position to play. I'd pencil him in for Chris Rogers' opening position, because while Rogers will be around for a while, he's older. I witnessed Hughes getting sawn off by bad umpiring decisions in India in

2013, and then missing out in terribly difficult conditions. Next time we give him a go, we should stick with him. He's a player for the future and I know he'll be hungry. He has eight to ten good years in him, and that could be 100 Test matches.

USMAN KHUWAJA IS an interesting case among our younger batsmen, and I think he needs to be more ruthless about the way he plays his cricket. This guy is so much better than a batting average of 25.13 in nine Test matches. He can look a million dollars at times, and he has a little bit of flamboyance or even flippancy about the way he plays. What I'd like to see is for him to be thinking, 'I need to tighten my game. I'm averaging 50 in first-class cricket and 25 in nine Tests and I can do better. What have I got to do? Maybe my shot selection needs work.'

I compare him with someone like Steve Waugh, who wasn't the finished article when he began playing for Australia either. He was brilliant at times, but he'd go through rough patches. Then as time passed, he toughened up. He realised he needed to play at 70 per cent of his capability 90 per cent of the time. That's where Usman is at. It's all there for him. The kid has it. Fortunately, he has Darren Lehmann's support, and Lehmann worked closely with him when he moved in as coach of Queensland, before his appointment as Australian coach.

Batting

Darren often talked about Usman's innings for Queensland in a Sheffield Shield match against Tasmania in the 2012–13 season at Bellerive, 138 on a wicked seaming strip when everyone else was struggling to reach 20. All that remains is for him to awaken himself, to become a professional cricketer, a hard-nosed player, and I really hope he does. He's a smart lad and I'd like to think he'll work it out. It would be a shame for him to be pottering around and only showing glimpses of brilliance.

WE'VE REACHED A point where we don't know which buttons to push with Shaun Marsh, who made a great century on debut against Sri Lanka at Pallekele in Kandy, in 2012, but who's been discarded since. We know he has the game to succeed but the crucial question remains: why hasn't he produced it more often?

Injuries are one reason, of course. He's been plagued by lower-back and hamstring injuries that appear to be connected, and he hasn't had a clear run. I feel very sorry for him on that front, because he's a great young fellow who used to hang around the nets with us for years when I was playing with his father, Geoff.

Still, I wouldn't write Shaun off. He's 31, but in the modern era this isn't the handicap it once was. Nowadays, with the improved professionalism of the modern player, with the attention to diet and fitness, many batsmen are still playing great cricket at 35. As a batsman, if your eyes haven't deteriorated you can play some of your best cricket well into your thirties. You're smarter and more aware of what you can do than when you were 25, and Chris Rogers is a great example of this. Brad Haddin is playing really well, too, approaching his 37th birthday. The way I see it, with the money that's available in cricket now, players will hang on longer, drive themselves to do so, and the 20-year-old will only be selected at the highest level if he's exceptional. I don't have a problem with that.

THE KEY TO batting is watching the ball, as simplistic as that might sound. It's the number one fundamental. Sometimes as a batsman you feel that you're watching the ball but in fact you might be looking at the general area or watching the bowler run in rather than watching it from the hand as you should. That's almost invariably the issue when you drift in and out of form. Are you watching the ball? Of course I am! But are you watching it right out of the hand? You have all your triggers with bowlers, things that tell you what they're trying to do. Sometimes you can work out what a bowler is about to do by the way he runs up, or the way he looks. Some batsmen will see something in a bowler's face, so it becomes important as the starting point to pick up as many signals as possible.

Batting

If you can pick it up out of the hand and read what the bowler's trying to do, it will give you that fraction of extra time to do what you need to. That's why it's always said that good players seem to have more time. It's because they pick the ball up quickly and their decision-making is good and clear—it kicks in as soon as the ball is released.

Foot movement is very important, and I constantly tell kids, 'Let the ball come to you and play as late as you possibly can. Don't go searching for it.' It's amazing how, when you're out of form, you start stretching for the ball out in front of you, but when you're playing well you let the ball come to you, which gives you an extra fraction of a second to get yourself into the right position.

The other thing I talk to kids about is not overplaying a shot. That might not be in the Twenty20 batting manual, but if you're playing grade cricket or long-form cricket, you should never overplay the shot and try to hit the ball too hard. You can hit it just as hard with timing and placement and getting your technique right. You can lose your shape, as they say, by trying to smash the ball.

While I'd argue that in long-form cricket batting hasn't changed all that much over the years, there have been big changes in 50-over cricket, with evolving tactics, higher scores, bigger bats and shorter boundaries. Twenty20 cricket is a new form altogether, where you're required to improvise and throw more caution to the wind. But

I'd argue that the basics are still solid for all forms: watch the ball out of the hand, let the ball come to you, move your feet and execute the shot.

BATSMEN NEED TO work out what they're good at, and what they can manage. My cutting and pulling came from my origins as a baseballer. My grip was wider, and my hands were apart on the bat rather than traditionally tight together, although I fiddled with those things over the years. With batting in cricket, as you find out in the process, you have to bat smart, understanding what you're best at and playing accordingly.

Good players stick to their strengths and avoid their weaknesses. They'll have a couple of big shots, just as Chris Rogers, for instance, has a cover drive and a cut shot, as do a lot of left-handers. If you wait for those few big shots and then accumulate in other areas—work the ball off your hip, nudge and nick it around—you really can score lots of runs. If they keep bowling to your cut and your cover drive, then you score heavily. A few guys have more options, on both sides of the wicket, and the best players have even more, but a lot of guys have three or four shots tops, with a few variations.

You'll find as you work through the ranks that at the highest levels you don't get many loose deliveries. Good bowlers will analyse how you play and try to take your strengths away. They can analyse quite deeply with the technology available nowadays, and the number of coaches. I take my hat off to the modern player, because the game has moved on. When I grew up, it was all about long-form cricket, and I developed a strategy around that. These days, blokes are expected and wanting to play shorter-form cricket, too, so they have to add strategies for those games. It can then become difficult to chop and change between the different forms.

Obviously you want to improve in your weak areas, which is a process in itself, but sometimes, why fight it? If it's not in you to be a hooker, why hook? Of course that's a shot you need now in one-day and Twenty20 cricket, because they'll bowl two bouncers an over at you.

You can get paralysis by analysis, there's no doubt. You can overcomplicate batting, and like in a lot of sports, players can start looking for those percentage points of improvement. But I counsel young people to keep it as simple as possible: 'See the ball, hit the ball.' Is there a better way of picking up what the bowler is doing? Is there a better way of hitting the ball? In modern cricket there are so many coaches and advisers around a team, with the focus on physical fitness and the body and the sports science, but the reality of the game is that you'll succeed if you keep it simple, see the ball and hit the ball. Look at Glenn McGrath's method as a bowler, prising out batsmen with line and length and persistence.

The best batsmen keep it very simple, and that comes through training and execution. Ultimately, you end up reacting without thinking too much. Sure, you'll need to make adjustments. On day one of a Test, for instance, the bowling and the surface will be a certain way, and you'll have to make subtle changes to factor in seam movement and steep bounce. By day five, the surface will have changed a lot, with footmarks and cracks in the surface, and sharp spin a possibility. On day one, the wicket might be flat enough that you can play your full array of shots. By day five, it might be up and down, turning, very difficult, so you'll need to put away a few shots. But the basics are always the same: watch the ball, use your feet and so on.

Good players can adjust to play well on different surfaces and in different conditions—that's what batsmanship is. In any one match, you generally have to adjust over the course of the game. You certainly have to adapt to different countries. And you need your strengths to fall back upon.

CONDITIONS PLAY A big part in batting technique. In England, for instance, you have to be aware that you'll play and miss, which is better than playing and nicking! The ball moves off the deck, so you rein in your shot selection if it's nipping around. You won't play as many big, expansive cover drives if the ball is seaming off the pitch, but you will put some shots away and try to get through while it's moving. Generally, over a five-day game, at some point you'll get the chance to capitalise and play all your shots.

The same principles will apply, however. Playing late is really important on a seaming wicket, but shot selection becomes an extra ingredient. That ball might be in your zone to cover drive but the risk–reward factor isn't in your favour because the ball's moving around. If it's not swinging and not seaming, then obviously you can play a more expansive game. That's what it's about, expanding and contracting to suit the conditions, and your team's situation: 'We're 4–30, do I go out and slog? I might try to occupy the crease for a while.'

On the subcontinent, of course, you get good spinners and turning wickets, which makes it tough. Everyone says you should have a technique to cover that, but every ball is unpredictable, because there might be footmarks that make the ball behave in extraordinary ways. You play as late as possible, use your feet and use your pad a little more strategically. A lot of guys prefer to keep the bat behind the pad, but I wasn't one of them. I preferred to have the bat out in front of the pad, because when the bat's in close you can pop up a lot of bat-pad catches. That was my method: to get to the pitch of the ball and stretch well forward with the bat in front of the pad.

The hardest spinner to play for me as a left-hander was the guy bowling into the footmarks outside the off stump.

Mind you, I preferred the ball spinning away to it spinning in, which is when you have to use your pad. A few guys gave me trouble like that: England's Phil Edmonds was difficult, as was Dilip Doshi from India. I only faced Bishan Bedi, the Indian genius, as a young man, and he was as brilliant as his off-spinning compatriots Erapalli Prasanna and Srinivas Venkataraghavan. Pakistan had Abdul Qadir as a leg-spinner and Tauseef Ahmed, who turned it the other way. Qadir was hard to read and very difficult to play in Pakistan; he wasn't so hard in Australia, but he was still top-shelf.

Most good players can read wrong 'uns or googlies if they watch closely. You watch the ball come from the hand, then you see which way the ball is spinning in the air. Then again, some wrist-spinners can be difficult to pick, like Brad Hogg, who had a terrific wrong 'un because there wasn't much difference in the release. Michael Bevan, also a left-armer with a fast action, had a good wrong 'un and, like Hogg, he could be hard to read, especially if you hadn't seen that type of so-called 'Chinaman' bowling very often. Shane Warne had a wrong 'un, but it wasn't as difficult to read, and after his shoulder injury he found it hard to bowl later in his career. But Warne had other variations, which goes to show that a great spinner doesn't need a big wrong 'un to prosper. In fact, the straight-on ball was probably Warne's biggest weapon.

•

Batting

THE CONDITIONS AT the WACA Ground in Perth are unique. At the WACA we used to talk about 'leaving on length'—basically, letting the ball go over the stumps—which the Western Australian guys were very good at. The principle was that any ball shorter than, say, a half-volley would bounce over the stumps, so you could let it go, even if it was heading straight over the middle stump. You wouldn't be out lbw unless it was a yorker! You need to let the ball go, which sounds ridiculous in a batting sense, but if you can do that and get yourself set, it becomes a great place to bat.

At the WACA, the ball comes onto the bat, your timing is accentuated and the sweet spot on the bat feels bigger. The cut is a big weapon there, and it's a great place to drive if the bowlers overpitch. Then again, if you nick it, the ball carries, and the slippers have extra time to see it. The WACA gives everyone a chance; even the spinners can use the sea breeze that comes in during the afternoon. But I never played in a winning team against the West Indians there, and I made my only 'pair' there in 1992–93. Their batsmen liked the pace and bounce and their bowlers were virtually unplayable.

On a dodgy wicket, one where the bounce is uneven, batting becomes a process. You have reduced scoring opportunities because if you play expansive shots, you're more easily dismissed. So it's about swallowing your pride a bit, digging in, and waiting for a rank ball. If you cut on an up-and-down pitch you can chop the ball on, for instance, so it's about accumulating runs to suit the conditions, expanding and contracting. You might need to do that even in the middle of a particular period, when there's a change of bowler and the game alters. You might have been seeing the ball like a football, but all of a sudden it's a struggle. This used to happen, for example, when Malcolm Marshall came back into the attack. As a batsman, you have to *sense* that change happening.

Mental application is very important, and it becomes more so the higher the level you play. Some guys are brilliant in the nets but can't convert it in the middle, whether it's the pressure or bad shot selection. You can practise as much as you want, but it's a different ball game out there. Your brain is trained to react, and you have your own triggers—like 'Watch the ball' or 'Use your feet' or 'Backlift!' or just a movement—but you don't want to be thinking too much or using too many triggers. You're better off having a single trigger, and then you'll react naturally to whatever's bowled. That's the hard thing. Your instincts are to hit the ball, but it might be a pitch where you can't use those shots. So you need to analyse what's happening around you, process it. With batting, there's a constant mental battle. You've practised to play a certain shot to a certain delivery, but in some conditions, that might not be possible.

Between balls, it's important to switch off, perhaps have a chat with your batting partner. Your concentration should only be engaged for the five or ten seconds it's required: 'Where's the ball? What are my triggers?' It can be difficult to achieve that few moments of peace between balls, because it's hard to think about anything else if a bowler is getting stuck into you—you're certainly not thinking about a day at the beach! In that case, you might think about the field they've set, whether there's a gap here or there. Of course, you're still analysing the state of the game, but it's not what I'd call total concentration. Not until the bowler starts running in.

Against the West Indians at their best, the physical fear factor was always there, but it was how you dealt with it that mattered. That's absolutely the key: you acknowledge the fear, then try to deal with it. You're thinking that the ball can hurt you, but the reality is, the *thought* of getting hit is worse than actually getting hit.

GETTING HIT IS an occupational hazard for a batsman. Players need to get their heads around that if they want to succeed. If you can find a way to put the fear to one side, you're halfway there. Obviously there are bad injuries, awful incidents where a player might be hit flush on the mouth or on the elbow, where it really hurts, but it's the *fear* that causes batsmen to make silly decisions.

In cricket, the secret is to put that fear to one side and focus. Batsmen who allow the fear to overcome them make bad decisions. You can lose your footwork and your focus, and the brain can play tricks on you against the pace of someone like Mitchell Johnson. And once your brain and your feet are out of sync, you're in trouble. That's why Johnson was so compelling against England in the Ashes series of 2013–14. He got into the English players' heads with pace, bounce and aggression, and the results— 37 wickets—speak for themselves.

I copped plenty of hits in my career, but only a couple of really bad ones. The English fast bowler Graham Dilley whacked me above the eye at the WACA Ground in a Test match in the summer of 1979–80, when I was 109 not out, up and running. I wasn't wearing a helmet that day, which sounds crazy in the current era, but it was the period where helmets were becoming popular but not necessarily compulsory, and while I'd worn one in the same season against the West Indian quicks, I didn't deem it to be necessary against England. But Dilley was sharp, I tried to hook him and missed it, and he drew blood. I had to retire hurt; I came back later but I didn't last too long.

I was hit on the back of the head by Dennis Lillee in a Sheffield Shield match at the Gabba in the early eighties, just ducking into a short ball. I was out to the next ball, trying to hook Dennis because I was a bit testy after the belt on the scone! When I came into the dressing rooms and threw my cap down, it was full of blood. I ended up having a few stitches from that blow. During my career

Batting

I broke or chipped all my fingers on both hands and my left thumb, which Malcolm Marshall rearranged for me.

The Victorian fast bowler Brad Williams chipped a bone in my right forearm in a Shield match at the MCG late in my career, and I had to retire hurt. I couldn't clench my fist or grip the bat, and I thought that I was in terrible trouble. But I was able to bat in the second innings using an arm guard. Joel Garner broke one of my ribs in a one-dayer at the SCG. To be honest, I'd been hit in the ribcage many times and, while it hurt this time, I didn't think much about it. I only found out that it was broken a bit later in that series when I dropped a catch, hurt a finger and had to go for an X-ray. While I was with the medicos I asked them to check my rib, and it turned out to be fractured, although it was more annoying than anything else, a bit like having a haematoma. We all endured plenty of those playing against the West Indians in that era, especially on the inside of the leg.

When I did wear a helmet, it had two temple guards but no grille. The only exception was in one Test series against the West Indies where I'd been playing poorly and they were peppering me with short-pitched bowling. I decided I was going to have to hook them, so I added the grille to the helmet in case I missed one. Nowadays you wouldn't think twice about donning the full kit, and the helmets are much better. I didn't wear a chest guard, either, but funnily enough, the worst injury I ever suffered in sport was at baseball, and I wasn't even playing! When I was a kid,

I was hanging around the baseballers over at Mosman oval and Johnno, my brother, distracted me for an instant. Just as I turned away, a foul ball decked me, breaking my jaw.

MY PEAK PERIOD as a player was from 1983 to 1987. If you have some determination and some skills, and you're playing against the same people day in, day out, you get used to fast bowling. It's never comfortable, but you do grow accustomed to it. Against the West Indian quicks, it was a war of attrition for me.

My first experience of facing them was in 1979 at home. They had Michael Holding, Joel Garner, Colin Croft and Andy Roberts, all great bowlers, and I felt out of my depth. Of all the West Indians, I rated Malcolm Marshall the best, although Curtly Ambrose could bowl long spells and he had awkward angles from his great height. But Marshall could be nasty and he could bowl on all surfaces, ramping it up or down depending on what was required. He'd bowl fast for five overs but he could bowl ten if required, and I loved the way he got wickets in Pakistan and India, which are usually graveyards for quick bowlers.

Holding was quick through the air and so rhythmic with his action, but as a batsman you could get into a bit better rhythm against him than some of the others. Garner's height made him difficult, and he could ramp it up too. Normally Joel might be fast–medium, late 130s to 140-plus km/h, but then he could find some extra pace if he was annoyed about something. Any time the clock goes past 140, it's quick. Then there was Croft, who was unusual. He bowled with his front foot splayed out wide and he'd angle the ball across me as a left-hander. Every over was a different challenge when you played against the West Indies. There was no respite, which was part of their secret. They were a special group.

I used to get a lot of short stuff from them, and generally I tried to get out of the way. I'd occasionally play the hook but I wasn't totally convincing with that shot. I'd look for the cut shot when the opportunity was there, and I might hit down the ground, because generally the field was behind me. I didn't have the swashbuckling stroke play, so for me, it was a war of attrition: bat for time, wear them down as best you can and gradually accumulate runs. It sometimes worked for me. My average was down against them, as it was for most guys (39.46 against a career Test average of 50.56), although I got some big runs on the 1984 tour of the Caribbean.

I know that India's Sunil Gavaskar thrived against them and Graham Gooch extracted a lot of runs for England against the West Indians, but they were exceptions rather than the rule. It was a relentless barrage, particularly when we faced them in Australia. Our wickets were perfect for them to play on, apart from Sydney, where it turned. I preferred to face them in the West Indies rather than here, because the wickets weren't as bouncy in the Caribbean.

You'd bat for time, squirt it around, play a couple of shots, pull a couple of shots out of the bag. I never thought I could hook consistently against them. It wasn't my game, counterattacking like that. I had to bat for time and take whatever opportunities I could during that time.

SOME GUYS ARE obsessed with technical stuff as batsmen, while others are 'see it, hit it' players. But even the more natural players will work hard in the nets—they don't just turn up at the match to have a bat. The Sheffield Shield has traditionally been good for us in this sense, because after an intense game you have a gap when you're at home and you can go back to the drawing board. But that's becoming blurred now as we play more cricket and the gaps in the schedule disappear. A few of the guys would have an eight-week break around Christmas, when the Big Bash League is played, but that can also be a disadvantage for a batsman, because you might be in great form and then have nothing but club cricket for two months.

Batting for a long time is an acquired skill. It's about building a score. I've heard people talk about going through processes or gears. You start off in first gear, you work up to sixth gear and then you're really flying. You then move up and down the gears depending on the bowling. You're in a good space if you're batting for time—it's a great feeling when you've been there for an hour and you're

Batting

20 or 30 not out. It's fun, but you can also lose concentration at the breaks or when you reach a milestone, which can be dangerous. At the top level, I think most players understand that when you already have a few runs—say, a half-century—it's time to cash in. It doesn't always work that way, of course. You might make a mental error through fatigue, and getting out between 100 and 110 is the most annoying thing—although you can get out to a good ball when you're one or 101! You should really push on when you get a hundred, because that's a great time to bat.

I WASN'T MUCH of a bat-thrower or into tantrums, like some players, but I've seen blokes who would come into the dressing room and hurl things about the place. Michael Bevan's antics had their own nickname—the *Bev Attack*—they became so famous, and he was but one of many.

I had one extremely embarrassing incident during a Test for Australia, at the WACA Ground against England in 1979. The dressing rooms were side by side, and for the Test match we were obviously using the home rooms, whereas when I'd played Shield for New South Wales against Western Australia we'd used the visitors' rooms. I was given out lbw to Ian Botham and was less than happy with the decision. I only just held it together as I walked off the ground thinking, 'Fucking Botham!' It welled up in me as I marched into the rooms, hurled my bat down, threw away my gloves and started carrying on and yelling, 'Pommy bastards!' I was in a blind rage but then I suddenly had a feeling that something wasn't right. I looked around and saw I'd walked into the wrong dressing room, the English rooms!

David 'Bluey' Bairstow, England's reserve keeper, was there, along with some of their extra players and their management. They were all just looking at me, cowering, probably wondering what this mad Australian would do next. It was an awful moment, and I had to pick up my bat, retrieve my gloves as quickly as possible and make my way to the correct dressing room, apologising appropriately. Then I copped it from my own guys: 'What were you doing, A.B.? Were you in there punching people in the opposition rooms?' I copped plenty of stick that night.

Any time I got out, I was a no-go zone for ten minutes or so. I didn't like people coming up to me, fussing around: 'Do you want a drink?' I used to hate that, and I had a few 'Captain Grumpy' moments: 'I'll get my own fucking drink!' I felt sorry for the attendants or the 12th man, because they'd probably been told to ask me. But give me ten minutes, and I was fine.

BATTING WITH TAIL-ENDERS was a mixed bag for me. On one famous occasion, the Test against England in Melbourne in 1982–83, Jeff Thomson and I managed to get within a breath of winning before 'Thommo' nicked one to slip. Thommo was sensational; he batted 129 minutes under pressure for his 21, and we put on 70. We lost by three runs in what people called one of the all-time best Test matches.

My process in those situations was to think to myself, 'I'm the last recognised batsman and nine-ten-jack will be here soon, do I start to hit out?' I found it was best to talk to the other player: 'Okay, another ten or 15 runs for us as a pair will be handy, and if we do that three times, it's very useful. We might get from 250 to 300, which is totally different.' It's about empowerment. In my experience, tail-enders tend to bat like tail-enders when they play with each other—have a slog and get out—yet when they bat with a recognised batsman, they tend to try harder, even down to Glenn McGrath, who would try his backside off. And tail-end runs are debilitating for an opposing team. It's amazing how much grief an extra 30 or 40 runs causes the opposition, how different the mood is in the dressing room with that little bit of cream on top.

Mike Whitney's guts and determination with the bat against New Zealand at the MCG in the 1987–88 season won a series for us when victories had been few and far between. We were 1–0 up in the three-Test series coming to the final match, and New Zealand set us 247 to win on the final day. Richard Hadlee was magnificent, and we'd slipped to 9–227 when 'Whit', another genuine No. 11, walked out to bat. Craig McDermott also held on strongly, but Whitney had the strike when the ball was thrown to Hadlee for the final over of the final day. Theoretically, it was a mismatch; Hadlee already had 10 wickets for the match. I'll never forget the roar of the crowd with each ball Whit kept out, one by one, until we'd drawn the match and won the series. He was a competitor, Whit, and he stepped up that day.

Bowlers who can't bat are an intriguing part of cricket, although the same is true of batsmen who can't bowl. It's remarkable to think that in the same game the separate skills could be so far apart. You think about a fast bowler of the excellence of Glenn McGrath, who ended up averaging 7.36 in Test cricket for Australia! Or Chris Martin, the fine New Zealand swing bowler who scored 36 Test ducks. Or Courtney Walsh of the West Indies, who at one point held the world record for wickets taken but also made a world-record 43 ducks!

I can also think of batsmen who were incredibly, embarrassingly bad with the ball in hand. If you'd said to Mark Taylor, for instance, 'You're not allowed to bat, and we'll grade your performance on bowling only,' he'd be lucky to play fifth grade. Geoff Marsh might sneak into the fourths, and David Boon into the thirds or seconds. It's a quirky game, no doubt about that. I'm lucky those blokes don't have right of reply here!

•

Batting

As far as stroke play goes, my best innings was 196 at Lord's in 1985 against England. I batted as well as I ever have, dominated their bowling and technically I played all the shots. I gave a chance early on, when I flicked a ball from Phil Edmonds into Mike Gatting's stomach in close. It all happened in slow motion as he had it, lost it, had it again then dropped it when I was almost halfway off the field. Taking the reprieve with thanks, I went on to play well, which was gratifying at Lord's, my all-time favourite ground.

Lord's is unique. If you make a century or take a five-for, they put your name up on an honour board in the away dressing room and it's there forever. When you walk out onto the field you start off upstairs, come out into the members' area where blokes are basically barging past you to go to the toilet, and you might have to say, 'Excuse me, I've got to go out and bat!' Then it's down through the Long Room and onto the ground. It's quite a daunting walk.

A lot of Australians share my love of that ground, and we used to play very well at Lord's, although not so much recently. In my time, we won there in 1985, 1989 and 1993, and drew there on the 1981 tour as well as in the Centenary Test in 1980. It's the mecca of cricket; it has a unique atmosphere and to play there is like a holy grail for Australians. I love the old-world charm of the place and its little quirks, like the slope that runs across the ground.

That century in 1985 was my best for stroke play, but probably my best innings in the truest sense was at Queen's Park in Port of Spain, Trinidad, in 1984 against the West Indies. I made 98 not out in the first innings against a quartet of quick bowlers—Joel Garner, Malcolm Marshall, Wayne Daniel and Milton Small—after we'd been sent in to bat on a difficult surface, reached 5–85 and were bordering on calamity. It was tricky with Garner bowling quickly, and it was overcast after a delayed start. Dean Jones, who was playing his first Test for Australia, came in at No. 7 and was squeezing the bat handle so hard I thought the glue would come out the top! I played and missed a bit, and I was hit a few times. 'Deano' played well and hung around for 48. I've heard him describe this as his best-ever innings, even though he later made two Test double centuries. That's how tough it was. Eventually we made 255 to put ourselves in the game, and I'd made my 98 not out in 360 minutes.

In the second innings our tail-end fell apart and I was up and running again. We were 5–115 at one stage and threatening to lose by an innings, but Terry Alderman managed to survive, in what I dare say was his best effort with the bat. From 9–238 at one point we ended up at 9–299, and he made 21 not out in 105 minutes. I'm not sure how he did it. As for me, I think I just focused harder when we were in trouble like that. The conditions were also a little easier, and I extracted 100 not out. I quite enjoyed playing in those circumstances where you just needed to drop anchor. What you have to say is, 'I can't do this from the dressing room. Being last man out is the only acceptable scenario.' You bat to a target and talk to the tail-enders: 'We've got to get a few more. Even if it's only 10 it could make a difference.' Then they knuckle down. I was quite proud of that Test, particularly the first innings.

I WAS NEVER motivated by records, but Adelaide in 1987 against New Zealand was a little special for me. It was a flat deck and everyone got runs. After the Kiwis piled up a big total, I made 205, my highest Test score. It was an eventful innings, because I could have been stumped at 57, and then at 66 Jeff Crowe, their captain, signalled 'no catch' when he seemed to have caught me at mid-on. In that innings I reached a century, then overtook Sir Leonard Hutton's Test total (6971), then Sir Donald Bradman's 6996 milestone. The following day I overhauled Greg Chappell's Australian record, 7110 runs, and reached my first double century.

Martin Crowe ended up having a light-hearted go at me with all the standing ovations the crowd was giving: 'For fuck's sake, A.B., are there any more records you can break?' He was being sarcastic but it was a little embarrassing, to be truthful, a fact I noted at the press conference that night: 'To pass Sir Donald's total is a great achievement, but you have to get it in its true perspective.

It's taken me nearly twice as long as the little fellow. It's just mind-boggling as to how good he must have been.'

I reached 10,000 runs, the second person to do so behind Sunil Gavaskar, in the Sydney Test against the West Indies in 1992–93. With the number of Test matches played now and a plethora of great players, that group has swelled to 11, with Sachin Tendulkar on top with a mammoth 15,921 runs. But at the time, it was a very exclusive group, and 'Sunny' sent me a fax welcoming me to the 'club'. It read:

> Congratulations, and welcome to the Club 10,000. It's good to have you as it was getting pretty lonely out here. For your information I'm sending you some of the rules of the club.
> - Membership is open only to players of restricted height and strokes—you have to be under five feet ten inches and you can't play the reverse sweep.
> - You must have taken at least one Test wicket.

IN CHRISTCHURCH IN 1993 against New Zealand, I finally overhauled Gavaskar's world record of 10,122 Test runs. It had become a bit of a media preoccupation and it was a little distracting, so I wanted it over and done with at Lancaster Park that week. I needed 50 and I made the runs by hitting Dipak Patel, the Kiwi off-spinner, to the leg-side boundary.

Batting

It was a little anticlimactic. Ian Healy, who was batting with me at the time, couldn't work out why I was celebrating a little; he thought I'd needed 57 for the record. I told him, 'I think that's it. I think I've gone past Sunny.' It was more of a relief than anything else, and I couldn't help thinking about Sir Richard Hadlee, who'd broken the Test bowling record a couple of years before in India, and had celebrated that night wearing a silk jacket and a turban and drinking champagne. Me? I had a couple of beers with the boys and scoffed some ice-cream cake that had been left in the freezer at the team hotel.

6

Coaching and Queensland

I UNDERSTOOD AUSTRALIA'S appointment of Mickey Arthur as national team coach in 2011. He'd had good results with his native South Africa, and he'd also done well as coach of Western Australia after moving to this country. Arthur beat out a field that included Andy Flower, the Zimbabwean who went on to coach England, and a few of my old teammates: Steve Rixon, Tom Moody and Justin Langer. He'd been at the helm of South Africa's team in 2008–09, when it became the first in 15 years to beat Australia in a Test series at home, the changing of the guard. Arthur had a good résumé and I get that, but having said that, *I* wouldn't have appointed him.

I believe we should have an Australian coach. We're a premier country in cricket, not a minnow like Bangladesh or

Zimbabwe, a top-ranked country if not *the* No. 1 country over history. So why would we need a coach from overseas? I heard Andrew Symonds say recently that he believed an Australian should be in the job, and I agree totally. Surely there'll always be someone in our very strong system who can do the job well.

I was disappointed with the Mickey Arthur period. I have nothing against him—he's a good coach and good bloke—but it just didn't work with our group. When Darren Lehmann replaced Mickey in 2013 after Cricket Australia decided it wasn't working, he had an almost immediate impact. It's a perfect fit, and Australia was back to the No. 1 Test and one-day international ranking within 12 months.

Good coaching is about communication skills. I dabbled in it myself—I coached Australia A for a time, and stood in as national coach for a short time on a tour of Zimbabwe—but never seriously. I just never saw myself doing that job nine to five, but to be a good career coach you need that drive. It's a job for a certain type of person. From my brief experience, it seems to be about cajoling the players and fostering a productive environment, a *winning* environment. You put in place certain criteria the players have to follow, and you ensure they're all singing from the same song sheet. Of course, that's not always easy when you have different characters within the team, but your communication needs to be strong and, in the end, you aim to create an environment where it's possible for all the players to find their best.

The best coaches do that, although they have different methods. You can be a Darren Lehmann type, adding a touch of humour with strong work ethic, drawing the players along and coaxing out their best, or you can be a really hard-nosed, no-nonsense type. You need to pick what fits that group of players and understand them, whether they need pushing and which buttons to push. It's an uncanny ability some people have; it separates the good from the rest.

WITH GOOD AND bad teams, it's incredible how often it comes down to having the right vibe; it means the players are out of bed, keen to get to the bus on time, and eager to practise and do the one-percenters, not grumbling about it or moaning about their lot in life. It's no longer a grind when a team gets into an environment like that.

As a coach, you have to say, 'Guys, this is the best time of your life! Don't you think the guy that's up at six in the morning to go and dig ditches would prefer to be a Test cricketer? Yes, it's hard work and there's pressure, but you guys are living the dream!' You want players to realise they're on a good wicket and can earn a seriously good living. Yes, they'll be away from home a bit, they'll miss their families and there's a certain price to pay, but you only do it till your mid-thirties at best, and then you have the rest of your life. As a coach, you want to engender that feeling that they need to make the most of it: 'I'm pretty lucky. Doing those extra laps around the oval or extra bowling when I'm tired, I mean, how hard is it?' That's the perspective they need.

The coach also has to make sure that certain issues don't fester in a team, because there are different characters in every side, and some of them sulk when they're not playing well. Each player needs to be cajoled in a certain way, or grabbed by the scruff of the neck and told it's time to move on. It's not just about technical instruction. You're trying to take away the peaks and troughs, to get things just flowing along nicely. The coach needs to know his players and recognise the signs of discontent or unhappiness.

IN MODERN CRICKET, there's a bunch of people around the group that take some of the pressures away from a captain, and you can debate whether it's good or bad. I often think a simpler system is the best system. Just recently I was watching a documentary on television with a lion cub in the zoo, and the handlers wanted it to swim. They threw it in the water not knowing if it would swim, but of course it did. Maybe that would be a good way for our young cricketers today.

Modern players are nursed along by a specialist batting or bowling coach, and a fielding coach, and a psychologist.

There seem to be endless crutches for them to lean on. I just wonder about the impact of that and I keep thinking about the lion swimming. I'm *not* saying we should go back to the old days, but it's that old debate: are you doing the right thing by your children if you buy them a car, or should you help them get a loan and then let them handle it? Are those people around the cricket team doing a good job? Yes, they probably are. But is it ideal for a cricketer who then finds himself out there in the middle, batting or bowling, with absolutely no one whispering in his ear? He doesn't have Dennis Lillee to help him with his technique when he's out there. It's up to him.

When things aren't going well, what do you fall back on? You go back to your coach and ask what was wrong. 'Well, your arm was too low,' he might say, or, 'Your backlift was going to point.' But you need to be your own coach to some extent. You need to know your own game. When you're out there, you have to analyse yourself, work out the conditions, analyse the bowler or the batsman and find a way to combat him.

Most players at the top level would have some help available, even back in the old days, but it was less formal. When I played, I used to talk to Greg Chappell at times, and I'd ask him to look at me in the nets. Prior to that, the senior players would do some impromptu coaching if you asked them to watch. Then in my time as captain in 1986, Bob Simpson came along as the Australian coach at the invitation of the ACB, and since then coaches have become a permanent appointment in all countries.

But are there currently *too many* people trying to help the players? To my mind, it's claustrophobic around the dressing room, but I guess the modern player is accustomed to that feeling. All the sports are doing it, and if it works and it converts to wins and better players, then I suppose it's justified. The Australian system has certainly headed that way, with a lot of specialists drafted in. Graeme Hick, the former England batsman, is at the National Cricket Centre (NCC, formerly the Australian Cricket Academy) in Brisbane now, Craig McDermott is in charge of the bowling, Shane Warne helps the spinners, and we have Greg Chappell overseeing high performance. That can't be a bad thing!

When I started we only had a manager, who was usually from the board and not necessarily a cricketer at all. It was sink or swim, which certainly does strengthen your resolve and character. At the end of the day, it's a fairly simple game, cricket, but players and coaches tend to complicate it. Sometimes the more people you have around a team trying to impart their expertise and justify their position, the more complicated it can get.

You want a happy medium with all this, because you do need coaches. The game has moved on from the old Ian Chappell edict that the coach wasn't necessary in top-level cricket, and that's especially so in the shorter forms.

•

Coaching and Queensland

THE RELATIONSHIP BETWEEN the coach and the captain is crucial. They don't have to be best buddies or agree on everything, but the relationship has to work. Bob Simpson and I were on the same wavelength as captain and coach. We worked well together from the time he came on board, and that's the kind of relationship you want.

Simmo and I had obviously played together, which probably helped, but our strengths and weaknesses were complementary. He was a strict disciplinarian, and he had an ethos of doing the basics well, which fitted with my philosophy. With cricket, you can add the extra layers and throw in your sports science and a few bells and whistles, but when things go wrong, you have to go back, find your basics and get them right. That's exactly what Bob Simpson did when we needed it.

We won the World Cup in India and Pakistan in 1987 not long after Bob started as coach, and he played a big role in that victory, which came at a time, not so long after the big retirements of Greg Chappell, Dennis Lillee and Rod Marsh, when we'd been flogged. Bob recognised that for us to succeed in that tournament, we had to be the best fielding team, and it's amazing how a good fielding team can be really difficult to beat. In that tournament we won three games by fewer than 10 runs, including the final over England at Kolkata by seven runs. When there are minuscule points of difference between the teams, excellent fielding can provide that winning margin.

Bob wasn't on the same page as certain players from his time, and he certainly had his critics, but we were a rabble when he joined us as manager–coach in New Zealand. My personal view is that Simmo was precisely what we needed at the time. He pared everything back, and the improvements came from there.

I DO WONDER whether we're falling behind because of our ethics. The batting coach Justin Langer recently said we need to have integrity and ethics when we teach our kids to bowl spin. I believe this is an admirable approach to coaching, but we're being left behind the rest of the world. The main issues are the 15-degree flex that's now allowed in bowlers' arms, a figure set by the ICC a few years ago; and the so-called doosra, the equivalent of a wrong 'un by an off-spinner.

It's fantastic to be ethical, but the game has actually changed. I get that we've taken the moral high ground, and I do question an individual's ability to bowl the doosra with what we used to regard as a normal, legal action. But is that old-fashioned thinking?

What's a throw? It was never written down, so in 2004 the ICC had a committee study the actions of various bowlers around the world, taking into account all the biomechanics. The issue had been jumping up a lot in the previous decade, since Muttiah Muralitharan was called for throwing, first by Australian umpire Darrell Hair at the MCG on Boxing Day 1995. In the old days, suspect bowlers were called on suspicion, from the Australian Ian Meckiff, who was no-balled for throwing in the sixties and taken out of the game, all the way to Muralitharan. But in this modern day of litigation, you'd only need a smart lawyer to pick up on the old rules: 'Hang on, you're banning my player, but where does it say what a throw is? Where does it say what a bowl is?'

When 'Murali' first came on the international scene he had a highly unusual action that most players thought was illegal. Then, when he started taking a lot of wickets, people started to say, 'Is this a legal action?' Murali underwent a barrage of tests and even went as far as putting a plastic guard over his elbow, but he does have a naturally crooked arm from a childhood accident. I've talked to him a lot, and he can bend his middle finger back onto the same forearm; he has incredibly supple wrists. So it might be that he's just a unique and special bowler.

Murali gets into awkward positions, and if you see his action frozen, he looks like a baseball pitcher. But does his arm straighten? It probably does, yes, but does it straighten more than 15 degrees? The ICC had the biomechanics people look at a lot of bowlers, and they all had a certain amount of flex. If you put a projectile at the end of a pipe and threw with it, then watched slowed-down vision of it, there'd be some flex, just as there is with a golf club shaft when you hit a golf ball. But under our old rules it was just 'Keep your arm straight', which the biomechanics people dismissed. They concluded, 'Just about everyone's arm isn't straight while they're bowling.' So what constitutes a throw?

That research back in 2004 was a watershed, because it found that under the old rules, most people were throwing. At that point the ICC had prescribed a 10-degree flex of the arm as normal, but even Glenn McGrath and Shaun Pollock, who were considered to have classical actions, occasionally went up to 12 degrees. At this point three biomechanics experts suggested that the human eye couldn't detect flex in a bowler's arm until it reached at least 15 degrees. They used cameras shooting 250 frames per second—ten times the speed of a standard television camera—to illustrate how the human eye can be 'tricked' when observing a bowler.

As a result of that research, the ICC set the limit at 15 degrees, and umpires and match officials were asked to note down any examples of suspicious bowling actions. A rehabilitation process was set up, and the ICC undertook to test bowlers at under-19 level so that suspicious actions could be picked up early, rather than when they reached the elite level. More recently, they've even had talks about using technology to monitor a bowler with a suspicious action while in competition. Certain bowlers in international cricket, such as Harbhajan Singh of India, have been ordered not to bowl their doosra after having been found to overstep the 15-degree limit. But it's difficult to police. How do you stop it in a World Cup final? The only way is for the umpires to call it if they see it.

In Australia, we've gone for the purest form of cricket, but it's like saying, 'You can't reverse sweep because you can't change your hands or your grip.' Nobody has stopped batsmen doing that. So if there's a blanket rule of being allowed up to 15 degrees before it's a throw, why not work to that?

I think we should be finding the guys who know how to bowl the doosra, like Saqlain Mushtaq, and getting them to show our bowlers how to do it. Then you test the kids and see if they're under 15 degrees. If they have a supple wrist and they can do it, then go ahead. We've been brought up with traditional views about how you bowl spin, and we don't want to be unethical, but is it time we acknowledged that the laws have changed?

It's like Adam Scott with his long putter in golf. It's still legal until 2016, and he wants to use it, so he uses it. It's no different from changes in the golf ball or the expansion of the heads of drivers in golf—all games evolve. I'd prefer that the traditional game be maintained, and the ICC might change the rules again, but until then, I'd contemplate going to the limit with our bowlers.

Cricket Australia announced recently that Muralitharan has been hired as a consultant to work with the national team and in particular with our spinners, and I applaud this move. I understand he's helping the spinners with grips and telling the likes of Nathan Lyon how he used to bowl the doosra. Lyon has tried to bowl a doosra, but says he can't manage it without exceeding the 15-degree limit. He does have, however, a ball—which he's called his 'Jeff'— that goes the opposite way to his off-spinner, although it's a work in progress. It will be fascinating to see what Nathan gets out of the relationship.

It would be fabulous if the likes of Lyon could learn to bowl the doosra, or at least some kind of off-spinner's wrong 'un, the kind that's been so successful for bowlers like Saeed Ajmal of Pakistan. If they can't manage the fully fledged doosra, then perhaps they can master the folded-finger delivery popularised by Ajantha Mendis of Sri Lanka a few years ago and known as the 'Carrom' ball—after the table game of the same name, popular on the subcontinent, where players flick a disc from their fingers. Ravi Ashwin of India has used the same ball but calls it a 'sodukku' ball, taken from a Hindi word.

The folded-finger deliveries have become popular but they're not new; Australia's Jack Iverson used the method in the fifties, and Johnny Gleeson, another Australian, copied it in the sixties and seventies. The principles are the same: you're creating a degree of uncertainty in the batsman's mind rather than sending down a succession of standard off-spinners. The batsman's thinking, 'How do I attack this bloke?' and is forced into defence.

Coaching and Queensland

It's great to have Murali on board, with his 800 Test wickets and 534 one-day international wickets to show for his craft. He's a wonderful character, although it would be virtually impossible for anyone to teach another bowler his style. He was unique, with his supple wrist and his permanently crooked right arm. I've been told he almost dislocates his right shoulder when he bowls, such is the degree of force and torque. All of this should be part of our efforts to encourage our team to play better cricket on the subcontinent.

I only played against Murali once, on the Sri Lankan tour in 1992, and I've never forgotten it. We played a board chairman's XI in a three-day tour match up at Kandy, Murali's home town, and he was only a young lad of 20. He confused me that day. I actually thought he was a leg-spinner, because of the motion of his wrist. He spun the ball massively, and to the first couple of deliveries, I had absolutely no idea. I was playing for the ball to spin back into me, as a left-hander, and I was missing them by miles. When I stumbled over to one and was almost stumped, I was thinking he had the best wrong 'un I'd ever seen. I was only awakened to the mysteries of Murali when Mark Waugh, who was batting at the other end, signalled to me, mimicking an off-spinning action: 'A.B.! *Off*-spinner! *Off*-spinner!' Murali made his Test debut a couple of weeks later in the second of three Tests, a series that was also Shane Warne's first tour for Australia.

Of course, Murali was dogged by controversy through most of his career because of his unusual action. Bob Simpson was among the first to raise concerns, telling the Sri Lankan authorities during that 1992 tour that Murali's action was suspicious, and that he might well be called by umpires when he travelled away from Sri Lanka. Nothing came of it, but the murmuring started soon after he began picking up big wickets at Test level.

On that Boxing Day 1995 at the MCG, Darrell Hair called Murali five times for throwing, the first time an umpire had taken action against him. Later that season Ross Emerson, another Australian umpire, also no-balled him, and a few years of controversy ensued. Murali was sent to the University of Western Australia for testing, and the biomechanists concluded his unusual action created the optical illusion that he was throwing. But that was scarcely the end of it.

My understanding is that Darrell Hair had written to the ICC several times before the 1995–96 series to say he had a problem with Murali's bowling action and to ask for advice as to what he should do. Darrell was acting on conscience; he believed that as an umpire he was bound to call a bowler he felt was breaking the law. But the ICC did nothing, of course, and Darrell ended up being the bad guy and was vilified. I felt for Darrell at that time, because he was a good umpire, a strong umpire, and he was left out to dry by the authorities. I also felt for Murali, who had a unique bowling action that was ultimately proven to be within the rules of the game.

I do maintain that his doosra was probably in breach of the rules, but in general he was legal. And he was a champion. He was an amazing competitor who played with a smile on his face, and he lived throughout his career with a huge amount of drama that would have made lesser guys turn up their toes. He never gave up; he went back to the testing procedures, got his clearances, and kept bowling and knocking batsmen over.

In hindsight, the ICC should have tested Murali earlier. He'd taken more than 80 Test wickets by the time Hair called him at the MCG that fateful day, and the Sri Lankan authorities were peeved that his action had been considered okay in some countries for several years yet was suddenly illegal in Australia. Fortunately, in the modern era, the authorities have made a point of picking out bowlers at under-17 and under-19 level if they believe their action is questionable. Umpires are also better supported. Sometimes it takes a major drama to sort out issues like that.

JOHN BUCHANAN WAS an absent-minded professor type of cricket coach but he's basically the reason cricket preparation is where it's at right now. 'Buch' took over as coach of Queensland towards the end of my career, in the 1994–95 season, and everyone knew he was different. We'd never seen a guy operate like that in cricket before. For an 'old-school' guy like me, it was quite challenging to cope with some of his ideas, but I remember thinking at the time, 'You know what? I'm going to give this guy a real chance.' I deliberately refused to question his methods too much, because as a senior player, I knew that some of the younger guys would be looking to see how I reacted.

John had been a very good club cricketer in Brisbane, and had played a few games for Queensland without being a star at that level, but he was very intelligent. He came in wanting to challenge traditional methods and structures, and I came around to the idea that just because the way he was talking wasn't traditional, that didn't mean it was wrong. In the end, he took cricket coaching to a new level, and people copied him around the world. He started the video analysis of players that has become commonplace nowadays. We had team meetings and analysed the opposition's players, and there was a structure to it. If we were playing Victoria, say, and we knew that Gary Watts hit anything short and wide, we'd have video of Gary Watts getting out, video of where he scored his runs, maybe something about how he was lbw the last three times he played. It was stone-age stuff compared with what they do now, and it could get a bit tedious. Computers weren't that great 20 years ago—and there wasn't even any Facebook!—but what they're doing now is done because of what John introduced.

He was at the cutting edge and it wasn't just about computers. He had a heavy focus on fitness, because he felt that cricket hadn't been strong enough on conditioning. He tried to address the drinking culture, and there were periods when we weren't allowed to have a beer until we'd drunk a bottle of water, and he introduced light beer, too. He revolutionised preparation for cricket and statistical analysis. You'd often see him sitting down at a game with a pad, writing in hieroglyphics. 'What are you collecting?' I might ask. He'd say, 'I don't know what I'm collecting, but I'm looking for patterns.' He had his detractors—I know Shane Warne wasn't a fan, and there were others—but he was trying to test the norm.

Buchanan took over as coach of Australia after he took Queensland to the drought-breaking Sheffield Shield win in 1994–95. It was a natural progression; he'd enjoyed success at the first-class level so it was time to try his methods in international cricket. He was a good appointment, and while he inherited a sensational team, I liked the fact he set out to make them better. They were already the best team in the world, but he challenged them to take further steps. John wanted to push the envelope with the players and the team, and make people as good as they could be.

The proof is there for everyone to see. Under Buchanan, Australia played some of the best cricket they've ever played and became a dominant team. He clicked with Steve Waugh as captain, and he brought other coaches into the system because he could see that was the way the game was going. He later went to England and into the county system, yet it didn't work for him there, or in New Zealand where he had a brief stint as national coaching coordinator.

It shows that John needed the right environment to get his messages across. I'm not too sure that the Kiwis and the English would take too well to an Australian telling them what to do and quoting Sun Yat-sen, the Chinese revolutionary leader, which he was apt to do. That was John. He was very good and he tried things that didn't always work. He wouldn't necessarily force them on you, but he was good at stretching the boundaries, collecting the data and finding jewels in the data. He changed the game in that way, and he'll forever be remembered as the coach of Queensland's first Shield-winning team. Talk about taking a gorilla off your back!

WE'D TRIED EVERYTHING in the Sunshine State to break the curse of the Sheffield Shield, from luring players like Wes Hall, Viv Richards, Majid Khan and Ian Botham, to bringing in players from interstate, like Jeff Thomson, Greg Chappell and me.

All manner of spanners went into our works, such as in the 1987–88 final in Perth, where Botham was detained by the police upon our arrival. He and I had an argument on the aeroplane before we landed. I'd been at a captains' meeting at Cricket Australia's offices in Melbourne, and I met the rest of the players at Tullamarine airport, where there'd been a few hours' delay and they'd been in the bar. There'd been a drama over food, and the Federal Police had been called, but they'd missed the players, who'd gone to get on the plane.

Then on the flight, some of the boys were listening to Billy Birmingham's latest 12th Man recording, which had just come out, reciting it at full decibels. I was sitting next to Ian Botham and Greg 'Fat Cat' Ritchie, who'd just been dropped from the Australian cricket team and replaced by Mike Veletta. We had a bit of an argument and Fat Cat was asking me, 'What role did you play?' It got heated, and Botham kept interjecting, 'Come on, you two.'

This went on for a few hours and I was dirty. When 'Beefy' interjected once again, I said, 'Bloody hell, Beef, will you just butt out!' We ended up having a push and shove with Fat Cat in the middle of us, and just then, the guy sitting in front with his young son turned around and said, 'Listen, guys, can you keep the language down?' Beefy grabbed him and said, 'It's got nothing to do with you, mate, turn around!' Beefy just lost it after that, and was in a foul mood, although I did notice that he apologised to the gentleman concerned before we landed, so I was under the impression that all was well.

When we arrived in Perth, the Federal Police met us and, after consulting with the flight attendants, took

Botham to the lock-up, right behind the WACA Ground, as it happened. When we tried to bail him out, they told us we needed a Perth resident to sign for him, so we called Dennis Lillee, who promptly arrived with a six-pack of beer! I was there with Ray Reynolds, our manager, and by then the world's media was onto it. In the end, we had to do interviews with the police at lunchtime of a day's play, so we probably did well to compete as well as we did. Western Australia won the final, and the drought continued for Queensland. Footnote: Beefy received a very small fine. The whole affair was a storm in a teacup.

We had a great group under Buchanan when we won the Sheffield Shield in 1994–95 for the first time. We'd been the laughing stock of Australian cricket, the chokers. I'd played in a handful of losing finals myself, but this time we'd qualified on top to have the final at the Gabba, meaning that South Australia, as the other finalists, needed to win. A draw would be enough for us.

We had a wonderful bowling attack and we knocked over South Australia for 214 then made 664 in our first innings to make it safe. We went on and closed out the match, and those scenes in the dressing rooms afterwards are etched in all of our minds. The song 'Holy Grail' by Hunters & Collectors had become our anthem for the season, appropriately enough, and it belted out of the ghetto-blaster in the rooms after the game. Old Queensland players like John Maclean, guys who'd been unable to shake off the curse, were coming into the rooms crying. That's how much it meant. We're bonded forever, that team, and we have a 20-year reunion planned for 2015. Everyone has aged a bit, but when we meet, it's as though we never stopped playing.

7

Touring

A LOT CHANGES in 35 years. The modern cricketer wouldn't think twice about taking a tour of India and the sub-continent, and I personally grew to love travelling there over three tours as a player as well as subsequent visits. But when I first toured India with a national team, in 1979, we'd heard horror stories from previous tours when the accommodation and facilities hadn't been good. Australia hadn't toured there for almost a decade, and there'd been crowd disturbances at three of the 1969 Tests, including a riot, as Australia won 3–1. Bill Lawry, the captain, called it the single toughest tour he took as a player, and Ashley Mallett said the team was made to stay in 'hovels rather than hotels'. At one point in Bombay (now Mumbai) the players actually stayed in accommodation at the ground.

So in 1979 when we toured under Kim Hughes' captaincy, we'd been indoctrinated in a negative way. I lived on naan and chicken and a few bananas, and lost a lot of weight. Some of our team were taping their mouths in the shower so as not to swallow any of the local water, which was considered dangerous. We didn't have any bottled water, so we had boiled water from an urn we carried around, and we drank the local soft drinks, Limca and Thums Up, out of bottles, and tea at the hotel. Nearly everyone had the belly troubles that were traditional back then, but the only one who didn't seem to get sick was Kim, who ate and drank everything! He'd say, 'What's wrong with you blokes?' Kim seemed to have a cast-iron stomach, and travelling in India certainly didn't bother him.

The umpiring was problematic. On that 1979 tour, the lbw decisions went 24 to nine against us, which made it very difficult to get on top. Nowadays, of course, all Test matches have neutral umpires, to take away that feeling of a conspiracy.

These days, the standard of Indian hotels and food is six-star, and it's a great place to tour. The grounds have improved out of sight, the infrastructure is in place, and cricketers are placed on a pedestal and feted. I reckon the rankings would go like this: 1. cricketers; 2. Bollywood stars; and downwards from there. Cricketers are right at the top of the tree.

Touring

But in 1979 our first experience of India was Madras (now Chennai), and the bus from the hotel went along the waterfront. At one point, we passed a big public-housing block with a large sign pasted on the side: 'To lose patience is to lose the battle.' Jim Higgs, the leg-spinner, took a photograph of that sign, and it became our mantra, in a way. The subcontinent has a vastly different culture, a different way of life, and it was a culture shock for us as Australians. Nowadays India is so much more westernised, the well-to-do Indian is very well educated, and it's a different ball game. When we arrived in 1979, there was chaos at the airport and cows wandering around and people everywhere, and we invariably drove through slums. We couldn't help but think, 'What have we got ourselves into here?'

The modern player thrives on touring India. It has become the centre of the cricket universe in recent years, and the likes of Brett Lee are immensely popular. Adam Gilchrist, Dean Jones and others do television commentary there, and the IPL competition is full of foreign players. If you talk about India being a tough tour, the Australian players look at you like you're from another planet. Of course, the underlying poverty is still there, but it's not as close to the tourist as it used to be, and the hotels and food are wonderful.

In 1979 the beer was terrible; now Kingfisher beer is great. Back then it was full of glycerine as a preservative, and the left-arm spinner Ray Bright had a trick where

he'd tip the bottle up into a glass of water and the glycerine would flow out. If you left the hotel in a place like
Calcutta (now Kolkata), there'd be tens of thousands of
people around the bus going crazy, held back by the army
guys with their lathi sticks. It was just hero-worship—they
loved Australian cricketers. They didn't want to hurt us,
they just wanted to touch us, be around us, and nothing
much has changed in that way. They're cricket crazy over
there, and the game has become a huge business. It would
be scary to work out the income it generates, including the
illegal betting, and all the gate receipts and the flow-on.
It would be a million times the rest of the cricket world's
income combined.

Occasionally there could be crowd troubles. At one
ground in 1979 the fans lit fires in the grandstand and
threw rocks in a mini-riot because rain and bad light were
preventing play. But I didn't feel threatened. We could
understand their agitation, especially given that in a lot of
these places people might have spent a week's salary on a
ticket to the cricket, and they quite understandably wanted
to see some play. There were situations where the authorities double-sold tickets, and you could be battling against
corruption and poor organisation. Overall I loved it there.
I found it a fascinating place and I loved their passion for
the game. Over the years, it has only become better as a
cricket destination.

●

Touring

ON THAT 1979 tour we went to Srinagar, a magnificent place in the disputed Kashmir region in the north-west, in the foothills of the Himalayas. Pakistan had a claim on the region and there had been several wars over it—the tensions exist to this day. As a team we'd been threatened by the Kashmir Liberation Front, and hence the security was very tight at the cricket ground and the hotel.

For reasons known only to me, I decided to play a stupid prank one night. I knew Kim Hughes' room was potentially accessible via his balcony, just along the way, so I came up with this idea of climbing out across my balcony along to Kim's and removing all his furniture while he was out. When security is so tight, you have to make your own fun!

I wasn't all that high up, but I started to make the climb across when boom, a spotlight hit me and I heard, 'Halt!' or whatever the Hindi equivalent is. Down below, two soldiers were pointing their rifles straight at me! I was so stunned I nearly fell, and of course it scared the hell out of me. I just yelled out, 'Australian cricketer! Australian cricketer!' It was very silly, but fortunately the security guards must have known we were all staying on the same floor.

IT TOOK ANOTHER seven years for us to tour India again, and by the time we went in 1986, I was the captain. We played some good cricket, and of course we played only the second *tied* Test match in the history of the game, at Madras, in the stifling heat of Chidambaram Stadium. That was a wonderful match, set up by our first innings of 574. Dean Jones made 210, in his most famous innings, and both David Boon and I made hundreds.

I'd been to India before, so I had some idea about the heat and humidity, but the 40-plus temperatures during that Test made it very tough for all of us. Jones batted for eight hours for his double hundred. When he was about 170, he wanted to go off. He was severely dehydrated and vomiting. I was batting with him and I knew Greg Ritchie was in next, but I wanted Deano to stay out there, so I said to him, 'Okay, mate, off you go. We'll get someone tough out here. We'll get a Queenslander!' I was just trying to fire him up, because he was batting so well. Of course I knew he was in a bad way, but who knew the extent of it? Who ever heard of dehydration back then? I soon found out! He told me to fuck off, kept batting and made those last 40 runs in a hurry, then collapsed in the dressing rooms so that the other players had to throw him into an ice bath. I was out soon after, and by then he'd been rushed to hospital. I thought, 'Bloody hell, I've killed him!' He was badly dehydrated, and you hear of people dying in that situation. He stayed in hospital overnight and thankfully was well enough to be released the next morning.

After four tough days of cricket, I declared and set India 348 to win, and in one of the most enthralling days ever, they almost got us. Late on day five, with India in a strong position, I thought, 'There's no justice. We've made all the running, and even so we're probably going to lose.' But thanks to some late heroics from the bowlers—particularly Greg Matthews, who trapped Maninder Singh lbw to end it all—the game finished in a tie. We ended up drawing that series and, as a group, we were on the way back. The core of that team—Geoff Marsh, David Boon, Jones, Steve Waugh, Craig McDermott—had come together, and we had some belief. We were no easybeats anymore.

WHEN WE WENT back to India for the World Cup in 1987, the team was gelling beautifully, and the experience of playing on the subcontinent just 12 months earlier helped. We were playing some terrific one-day cricket that would later cross over to the Test match arena. Bob Simpson prepared us relentlessly in the heat of Chennai, and we won the first game, against India, to set it up. Towards the end of our innings in that game, Dean Jones hit a ball over Ravi Shastri's head at long-on for what we knew was a six, but Dickie Bird, who was umpiring, asked Ravi whether it was four or six, and he signalled that it was four. We finished with 268 but Alan Crompton, our manager, went to see the match referee, Hanif Mohammad. They reviewed the decision made on Jones' shot, agreed it was a six and upgraded us to a final score of 270. All of which turned out to be incredibly important, considering India made 269. Steve Waugh finished it, bowling Maninder Singh. I think the cricketing gods were on our side that day!

Our method was to keep wickets in hand then slog at the end, and we tended to bat first whereas other teams were tending to chase if they had the choice. At 15 overs, we liked to be around 50. In modern cricket, of course, they'd like to be 50 after eight overs, but one-day cricket was evolving, and 240 or 250 was a decent total to defend in India. Nowadays, with the bigger bats and the ropes in, they'd be looking at more than 300 all the time. That's how much the game has changed.

When we went to Lahore for the semi-final against Pakistan, people were tipping we'd be carved up. The Pakistanis under Imran Khan's captaincy were a terrific side. We batted first and made 267. Steve Waugh took 18 from the last over of the innings, bowled by Saleem Jaffar, which put some pressure on the home team, and then in a boilover we bowled them out for 249 with Craig 'Billy' McDermott taking five wickets. We had beers in the change rooms, which was a bit unusual for Pakistan (I'm not sure who organised it, although I suspect it was the Australian Embassy crew who had turned up for the match). We also smuggled some beer onto the aircraft and headed for the final in Kolkata against England, who'd beaten India in the other semi-final.

Our all-rounder, Simon 'Scuba' O'Donnell, was suffering from non-Hodgkin's lymphoma, but none of the players knew, although he'd confided in Simmo on the eve of the final. O'Donnell had found two lumps on his ribs during the tournament, but he wasn't fully diagnosed until we returned home, so we played the final at Eden Gardens with no clue about Simon's life-threatening situation. I do remember that after the semi-final triumph he was a bit reserved. Usually Scuba was lively, and his go-to song was 'Billy Don't Be a Hero'. But he picked himself up for the final and bowled very well. He also made a full recovery from the disease and played wonderful cricket for Australia, especially at one-day level, for some years afterwards.

The Indians in the near-100,000 crowd supported us in the final, perhaps out of anti-Anglo sentiment, or because the English had beaten India in the other semi-final. The atmosphere was awesome and very much in our favour. We tried a few different tactics, particularly McDermott as a pinch-hitter, with some success, and Michael Veletta (45 off 31 balls) played brilliantly. Veletta was a fine one-day cricketer with some dinky shots, and he'd also played well in the semi-final. He was a great tourist and a brilliant fieldsman; he played a big part in our win.

We'd debated whether to play Tim May or Peter Taylor as the spinner, and 'Maysie' won that battle for a more attacking option, but he took some punishment from England in the final. As a consequence, I had a bowl with my left-arm spinners, not uncommon in one-day cricket.

I've reminded Mike Gatting about his reverse sweep to my very first ball, gloving a catch to wicketkeeper Greg Dyer, ever since! When we were setting the field, I was thinking, 'I want to bowl tight into his pads.' I set a strong leg-side field, because he was batting well at that time and he was a good sweeper. I had backward point, point, cover and mid-off, so he obviously thought there was room on the off side. I was a bit stiff bowling that first ball and actually pushed it wide—it might have been nearly 60 centimetres outside the leg stump—but 'Gatt' had premeditated the reverse sweep and, as a result, he had to reach for it. In doing so, he gloved it onto his shoulder and up in the air for Greg Dyer to take the catch.

It was a big wicket, one that turned the tide. We'd had our noses in front, but it was tight, and Allan Lamb was playing well for England. We ended up winning the World Cup by seven runs, jogging a lap of Eden Gardens with the trophy. It remains one of my favourite memories.

I DID 28 cricket tours, and England was my favourite. The cricket itself is fabulous, and I love the grounds. The pitches suited my game, with their lower bounce, and the crowds are knowledgeable and appreciative of good cricket. Logistically, you can get away from the cricket if you want to and become a bit of a tourist, and as a player you're travelling by luxury coach in a tracksuit rather than by aeroplane in your best attire. On most tours, you're in and out of a suit and at airports all the time, and it takes all day to get to where you're going.

By the time I made my first full tour of England with an Australian team in 1981, I'd enjoyed two seasons of league cricket and already loved playing in England. But the 1981 tour, of course, became known as 'Botham's Ashes' and it left horrible memories, at least of the cricket! We lost the series 3–1 but we should have won it. As a team we missed Greg Chappell, who along with Viv Richards was probably the best player in the world at the time, but he had personal and business reasons to miss the trip. When we had bad periods on that tour, they were terrible. Terry Alderman took 42 wickets in the Tests and Dennis Lillee took 39, a combined 81 wickets that should have seen us through, yet we still couldn't win. Our batting really let us down at the crunch times.

Headingley, Leeds, was the low point. When the golfer Doug Sanders was asked in an interview how often he thought about the short putt he missed to lose the British Open in 1970, he said, 'Only every day!' For us, the Leeds Test of 1981 is a bit like that. We had a 227-run first-innings lead, and pushed England to 7–135 in their second innings, but somehow—thanks to Botham and, with the ball, Bob Willis—they came back from nowhere and won. It was only the second time in Test history that a team had followed on and won a Test match. At tea on day four, they were gone. Botham had just come in, and the players had booked out of their hotel the night before to make the quick escape. A lot of us had been over to Botham's place on the evening of the rest day, and they knew they were in all sorts of strife.

At tea they were seven wickets down and we were cock-a-hoop. Up on the big screen at the ground, this graphic appeared: 'England 500–1 at Ladbrokes.' I think it was Dennis Lillee who said, 'I'll have a slice of that!' I'm not a gambler, but they were ridiculous odds in a two-horse race. We couldn't lose, surely. They were seven-down, still behind and it was a difficult wicket. I think Lillee initially wanted to have 50 quid on it, but he was howled down, of course: 'Why would you want to waste 50 quid?' He called over our bus driver at the time, Peter Tribe, whom we used to call 'The Geezer', and asked him to put £10 on England. I think Rod Marsh quietly said, 'Slip five on for me,' and Peter went to the Ladbrokes tent.

When he batted, Botham just swung from the two-bob seats, and it's amazing how, under pressure, you can *lose your shape*, as they say now. We lost our bowling tactics. He was swinging hard at everything, so we bowled a few bouncers at him, and started to lose our rhythm and lines and concentration. He was either swinging and connecting or swinging and missing, and then he started to connect really well, and the ball was flying through covers instead of over the slips. Their fast bowler Graham Dilley came in at No. 9 and batted like he was Graeme Pollock for one day in his life, carving out 56 and getting caught up in the groundswell of Botham's onslaught. We kept going to Lillee and Alderman thinking, 'Finish them off!' They gave it everything they had, but an hour and a half later the bowlers were exhausted. Tactically, we lost our way, because we thought Botham would eventually hit one up in the air.

Botham went crazy and made 149—England would have scored 130 or 140 in the last session—then on the next morning, he hit the first ball for four before Bob Willis, their last man, got out. We only needed 130 to win, but the mindset was suddenly different: 'How did we let the game get to this stage?' Bob Willis bowled like a man possessed; he was in the zone, bowling at his peak, making it lift awkwardly. At one stage we were 2–56 and John Dyson had batted well, but Graeme Wood was given out caught behind off the footmarks, and that hurt us. We wobbled, then fell over for 111. Actually, we were lucky to get that many. Even though everybody had given it their all we fell well short that day.

It's amazing to think that in the aftermath Marsh and Lillee collected £7500, but it's worth remembering that there was none of the furore over gambling in cricket that came to pass a bit more than a decade later. Dennis and Rod bought Peter the bus driver a set of golf clubs and a return air ticket to Australia. It was some consolation to them, but I know they would have preferred a win.

Botham terrorised us that season, and if he wasn't getting hundreds, he was taking his share of wickets. When you go to England, even nowadays, the television stations will show endless replays of that series when there's a stoppage in play. I've never, ever felt worse at the end of a game than I did in the pavilion at Leeds that day.

WE WERE PLAYING against Sussex on the 1985 Ashes tour when we were offered a few tickets to the FA Cup Final at Wembley. It was early in the tour, and I managed to roster myself off for the county game so all up five of us could jump on the train to London for the day. We put our blazers and ties on, unsure of the dress code for the area we'd be watching from, and we stood out like beacons once we got into the London tube system, packed as it was with Manchester United and Everton supporters in their colourful gear.

Then someone recognised us: 'It's Allan Border.' Then: 'It's the Aussie cricketers.' And at that moment, the whole trainload of soccer fans spontaneously started singing 'Tie Me Kangaroo Down, Sport'. It was a fantastic moment we'll never forget, albeit totally embarrassing! There's no sporting atmosphere better than British soccer.

BEFORE WE MADE it to England for the 1989 Ashes tour, one of my favourites, there was a bit of drama over David Boon, who was reputed to have consumed 52 cans of beer on the journey from Sydney to London, beating the previous record by an Australian cricketer, held by Rod Marsh. Boon has always denied the 52-can figure, although official record-keepers have it at that. I do know that I presented him with a gold-plated ring-pull, engraved with '52', at the end of the tour!

When we arrived in London, it was early morning and we had a big, grand press conference at our hotel, the Westbury, in Mayfair. All the players were to attend, and I had to introduce them one by one to the assembled British media. I can still remember sitting with Simmo and the manager, Laurie Sawle, and calling out, 'the five-foot-two Tasmanian with the flared pants', as 'Boonie' shuffled out into the spotlight. He took up a position right behind me and kept pulling my jacket, tipping me back on the chair, sticking his finger in my ear and being a pest, but he was upright at least.

His drinking exploits were to be kept under wraps, but of course Simmo found out, and at our first team meeting threatened an early trip home for any ill-discipline. He also told us this was to be kept in-house, upon which Merv Hughes piped up, 'Ahhh, Simmo, I might've let the cat out of the bag . . .' Merv was doing a regular radio spot and had already broken the news to his listeners back at home in Melbourne in his first segment! David was pretty quiet from then on—most of the time—and, after a great tour, ended up hitting the winning runs in the Old Trafford Test to give us the Ashes.

One of the funniest moments I've seen on a cricket field involved Boon on the same tour. On the day after we won the First Test against England at Leeds, we had to play Lancashire at Old Trafford in a county match, and we were the worse for wear after a huge celebration the night before. Leeds had been our bogey venue, so to have knocked over England and taken a 1–0 lead, particularly when they had a chance to draw on the final day, was massive. We bussed to Manchester immediately after the match, and went straight to a local bar, where Boonie, Tom Moody and others worked their way through the spirits, colour by colour, as a drinking game.

As a tour selector, I astutely stood aside for the Lancashire match and watched as the lads took on a team that included two seriously quick bowlers, Wasim Akram of Pakistan and Patrick Patterson of the West Indies. The Australian guys were a mess, some of them sleeping in the rooms as they waited to go onto the field. Boon was fielding at his normal position at bat-pad when one of the Lancastrians looped up a catch. Everyone yelled out, 'Boonie!' and, as he woke up, he started looking skyward to see where the ball was, upon which the helmet fell down over his eyes. Panic set in and David did some strange-looking pirouettes, desperately trying to recover his balance. The ball fell gently to earth in the end, almost hitting Boonie in the head as it dropped. The rest of the players couldn't help but laugh hysterically as the catch went down. In fact, Geoff Marsh, who was captain for that match, reputedly still had tears of laughter rolling down his cheeks when he dropped a catch a couple of overs later. But we won the match, which was a theme for that tour.

We won the series 4–0, and it was the first time since 1934 that an Australian team had gone to England and regained the Ashes, as opposed to holding on to the trophy. But people forget that it could easily have been 6–0 but for the rain and some digging in by Robin Smith, their best batsman in the series. We were well on top in the two drawn Tests, at Birmingham and at The Oval, but the weather prevented us from winning. When we came home, there was a ticker-tape parade for us in Sydney, which was a surreal feeling. As we were waiting in the cars, we were wondering if anyone would turn up, but sure enough, tens of thousands came out to see us that day.

Another great day in the aftermath of the 1989 Ashes tour was when the team was invited to the 1989 VFL Grand Final and I was asked to toss the coin. I was ushered out into the middle and introduced to Michael Tuck, the Hawthorn captain, who appeared as cool as a cucumber. I think, from memory, this was Hawthorn's seventh straight Grand Final appearance. The Hawthorn boys were just going through their warm-ups, all looking very calm. On the opposite side were Geelong captain Damian Bourke and his lads. Their mood was very different: their eyes were spinning, and their warm-ups were a lot more physical. The two captains came together and I said, 'Heads you win, Michael; tails it's you, Damian.' Up went the coin and it came down in Geelong's favour.

Now Damian Bourke is a big man, towering over me, and straight away he just extended his arm right past my nose, shouted, 'Fucking that way!' and stormed off. That was the end of the toss! I didn't know much about VFL, although I love the game, but I knew what was about to happen. I raced off the ground to where our boys were sitting and they immediately started asking what it was like. I said, 'Boys, there's going to be a fight!' Sure enough, the game exploded into action from the first bounce and went on to be what's still considered one of the great Grand Finals as well as one of the most brutal.

I MET A lot of famous people in my time playing for Australia, but I really came to admire elite sportspeople, I guess because, having played at the top level of cricket, I had an empathy and a feeling for the highs and lows and the sacrifices required. Sir Garry Sobers, the great West Indian all-rounder, was an early cricket hero, and I came to love Björn Borg, Sweden's magnificent tennis player. In fact, as players we came to know all the Australian tennis legends —such as Ken Rosewall and John Newcombe—because they'd often be staying at the Hilton in Melbourne when we were there for matches at the MCG.

I'm a 'leaguey' from way back, a big fan of the NRL. My earliest memories include watching the North Sydney Bears with Mark, my brother, snatching defeat from the jaws of victory. My favourite player was Ken Irvine, who holds the first-grade rugby league try-scoring record at 212 tries (although Billy Slater is sneaking up on him). I also met the likes of Reg Gasnier, Norm Provan and Johnny Raper, legends of the game.

I admire Greg Norman, and I met him many times and watched him play at the Masters in Augusta. I even went to play with him at his club, Medalist, in Florida, and stayed at his home at Jupiter Beach after a barbecue and a few drinks. Greg was great for Australia, and I hate the way people hacked him down at times because he lost a few big tournaments. I hate the term 'choker', because we all get nervous, whatever the level we play at and whatever the sport.

Greg lost majors several times because another player did something extraordinary. It's not choking when an opponent holes out from a bunker, like Bob Tway did, or chips in from 50 metres like Larry Mize. You could give Mize another hundred tries at that shot he hit at Augusta in 1987 and he wouldn't make it. When Greg lost at Augusta in 1996, the day Nick Faldo reeled him in from a six-shot deficit, I was watching on television like just about everyone else in Australia and feeling Greg's pain. I remember his iron shot to the ninth, a par-four, landing near the flag and then spinning back off the green and down the hill. It spun too much; that's not choking, it's bad luck.

I PROBABLY KNEW from some years ago that Adam Scott would be a superstar in golf, because I played with him when he was quite young and he did something I've never forgotten. I love my golf, and when I was invited to play in the pro-am for the Australian PGA Championship at the Coolum resort, they paired me with Adam. He was hitting the ball magnificently all day, and I was striking it reasonably well, too. When we got to the tenth tee, he said to me, 'This hole, let's have a long drive contest!' He'd been hitting it 50–100 metres past my ball, so I said, 'Sure, buddy, you're kidding!' Then he said, 'I'll use your club.'

Now I'm a left-hander at golf, just as I was at cricket, so this put a different light on his challenge. I've seen golfers hit shots on the opposite hand by inverting the club, which is handy sometimes if you're stuck behind a tree or beside a wall or a fence, but it was always going to be tough for him to do that with a driver, given its shape. I hit a decent shot and then handed him the club, expecting him to invert it and play right-handed.

But no, he set himself up on the opposite side of the ball, and had a nice practice swing, left-handed. It was like a mirror image of his beautiful right-handed golf swing. Then he smashed it about 50 metres past my drive. 'You're kidding,' I said. 'What's the story there?' He explained that when he'd played cricket as a boy, he'd been a left-handed batsman. 'So I have a bit of an advantage,' he said.

Scott wasn't done yet. When we walked up to his ball, I thought he'd pick it up, since he had another ball in play and it was only a practice round for him. But he asked his caddie for a yardage, then grabbed my left-handed eight iron out of my bag. 'Whack!' Up it goes onto the green. Now that's just not fair!

CRICKETERS ARE SUPERSTITIOUS, there's no doubt, although I was far from the worst. Terry Alderman, swing bowler supreme, was as bad as I've seen, and I even missed seeing some of the cricket on the 1989 Ashes tour because of Clem's obsession with staying in position.

The routine is that if a partnership is building while Australia bats, you don't under any circumstances change your position lest you cause the fall of a wicket. This has been happening in Australian cricket for a long time, and in 1989 we were involved in a tense run-chase at Lord's against England when I came back in from batting and headed for the shower. By the time I finished, we were gathering some momentum and Clem wouldn't allow me back onto the balcony to watch. This went on for some time, but there was no way anyone was allowed back onto that balcony. When we only needed a handful of runs to win, with plenty of wickets in hand, I finally received approval to take my place and watch, but that was only after hanging in the showers for about 90 minutes!

It goes further than that, of course. In our dressing room, you'd never say, 'Boonie's playing well,' or, 'Swampy's on fire'—that would be potentially putting the mocker on them. If a partnership was building and you needed to use the bathroom or get something to eat, it was imperative that you return to the same seat. It's taken very seriously, and if a wicket falls, you could be accused of causing the calamity. Clem was red-hot on it; he even reacted to the devil's numbers—87, the Australian curse, and even 111, which is 'Nelson' for the English.

I always put my right pad on first when I was preparing to bat, and I went through a phase when I didn't shave during Test matches, thanks to Björn Borg, who won five Wimbledon titles in a row from 1976 to 1980. I'd seen him say in an interview that he never shaved during the championships, so I followed this routine for a while. Once in Perth I had a function to attend in the evening, and I was a little scruffy, so I shaved, but the next day I was out early, and that was a lesson for me. I was back into the habit of not shaving and it lasted for years.

•

Touring

TOURING CAN BE really tough on a family, and it meant I missed the births of my first two children, Dene and Nicole. I was in the West Indies in 1984 when Dene, our first-born, came along. Of course, nowadays you'd fly back home to be there, but this was a different time, and I was in St Lucia about a fortnight away from coming home to Australia. Jane rang me and said, 'I'm going in. I'm in labour.' So I wished her luck, then sat awake in the hotel room until 3 am, waiting for another phone call, until I eventually nodded off. The phone rang and woke me in my room about 7 am and it was Jane to say, 'We had a baby boy!' I hadn't realised that the telephone exchange in St Lucia cut off at midnight, and we didn't have mobile phones in those days, so Jane had been unable to get through. Then we had to go through the process of getting a photograph through; with today's technology it would be five minutes at most, but back then it took most of the day.

When our second child, Nicole, was born, there was a chance I could make it for the birth. We were playing a Test match in Sydney, Jane was being induced, and plans were in place for me to be whisked away to Brisbane. But as it happened, the Test dragged on and I couldn't leave. Fortunately, I was there for the births of our third and fourth, Tara and Lachlan.

PAKISTAN WAS CHALLENGING as a player. I had three tours there, and I also took an under-19 Australian team there after I stopped playing, so I'm very familiar with it. On my first tour of Pakistan in 1980 I made a lot of runs, then in 1982 I had a shocker—I got the grumps and didn't enjoy it. For the First Test in 1980 the pitch was a raging turner, and we suspected a conspiracy had been hatched. What tends to happen on the subcontinent is that you play on a very spin-friendly surface first up, before you've had a chance to get used to the conditions. It's understandable and it's something we need to prepare for in the future. The Pakistanis were 1–0 up in the series coming to Lahore for the Third Test, and we had the great Dennis Lillee, who'd been blunted by the dry, turning, low-bounce tracks. When we arrived in Lahore needing a win to draw the series, it looked as though they had two pitches prepared, one greenish and one a belter, so we tried to bluff our way through it. We asked Dennis to fake an injury, and he responded by running into the nets and completely overacting his part, carted off with an apparent back injury!

We wanted them to think, 'No Lillee, no Australia,' and be duped into choosing the greener pitch to play on, because they did have Imran Khan and Sarfraz Nawaz to bowl seam. Sadly, they never fell for the trick: the pitch was a belter, and as a result I scored 150 in each innings. There should be more pitches like that one! But it was another draw, and Dennis left Pakistan with three wickets for the three-Test series, a rare tough tour for him.

Touring

In Pakistan, you see some odd things at the cricket. One morning when I was batting in the nets, which were on the ground, Imran came up and asked me if I'd mind if he had a bowl at me. I was a bit surprised but agreed, and that's the only time I can ever remember an opposing player bowling at me in a net during a match. He explained later that he didn't particularly like bowling to just a stump and preferred to have a batsman there so as to get his lines and lengths right. The nets weren't great, but it was great fun!

You make what you can of being in Pakistan, because you're confined to quarters a little when you're there. We took this a little too far in 1988 in Lahore, when Greg Ritchie, who was a first-time tourist, was involved. Out of boredom we'd taken to buying fireworks we'd discovered for sale in the old part of town, and blowing them up in strategic places, such as teammates' rooms. We were all on the same floor at the hotel, and we'd sneak a cracker under someone's door and scare the hell out of him.

Then the hotel management took exception, presumably after a number of complaints, and the tour manager, Fred Bennett, ordered no more fireworks. This led to the invention of the delayed fuse, which consisted of a cigarette with the wick pushed in partway down, meaning it could be lit and the offenders escape the scene before the firework exploded. So we could be in Fred Bennett's room, if we so desired, when the explosion occurred in a teammate's room, and feign total innocence. This tactic went on for a while until Fred said enough was enough and threatened a firing squad if any more crackers went off.

After we used all the purchased fireworks we were left with one huge rocket with a massive head and a sort of tomato stake attached, and it was just teasing us, sitting there in Fat Cat's cupboard. One night there was a big wedding downstairs beside the pool area of our hotel, and Fat Cat decided to provide the wedding party with a little surprise fireworks display. He set up the rocket in a soft-drink bottle perched on the balcony outside our room on the seventh floor, the idea being that the rocket would explode in the sky above the crowd. But it all went horribly wrong. The bottle tipped over as the wick burned down, and sparks started to fly. The missile whooshed at a horrible angle straight above the heads of the assembled guests. I reckon the Pakistanis must have thought neighbouring India was attacking, such was their surprise, and we commando-crawled back to our rooms to escape scrutiny. I'm still amazed that we escaped capital punishment!

THE TERRORIST ATTACK on the Sri Lankan cricket team and other officials in 2009 at Lahore changed everything for cricket, apart from being a terrible tragedy in which six policemen and two civilians were killed and many others injured, including six of the Sri Lankan team. As the Sri Lankans were en route to Gaddafi Stadium for a Test match, with the umpires and match officials in convoy—including Australian umpires Steve Davis and Simon Taufel as well as Australian coach Trevor Bayliss, who was in charge of the Sri Lankans at the time—they were fired upon by Kashmiri militants.

Who would have thought cricket would be a target for terrorists? As it was, teams had been refusing to play in Pakistan for a few years before that, and the Sri Lankans had been through some debate before agreeing to travel there. I doubt whether an Australian team will go back to Pakistan, which is a shame, but people are prepared to do anything to have their grievance aired now. When I played, we'd have armed security on our floor, but we never felt threatened. We didn't have to check in and out of a hotel each time we left, as they do now. That single incident has changed the landscape of the game forever.

THE TOUR OF the Caribbean is tricky as a player, because the West Indies constituents are different countries with separate currencies, and getting to another island can be an all-day event. But the islands themselves, such as Antigua, Barbados and St Lucia, are idyllic—it's a bit like playing cricket on Hamilton Island. The grounds are small, but the crowds are knowledgeable and can get feisty, too. There'll be reggae music playing and a unique atmosphere in the crowd.

In my time of going to the West Indies, the cricket was tough, of course. They were an outstanding team in 1984 and 1991, brimming with quick bowlers, and we'd spend the day ducking and weaving, trying to scratch out a score. Even the small island teams had young blokes trying to make a name for themselves. What's happened to West Indies cricket over the last few years is sad. They seem to focus on shorter forms of cricket, and the production line of talented fast bowlers has closed down. Young athletes seem to be gravitating to other sports, such as athletics and soccer, or trying to get college scholarships in the United States, and that has had an impact on their cricket.

Cricket is the only thing they do collectively in that part of the world, and within their cricket there can be dramas between the different cultures, the different islands, so to get everyone firing together as one can be difficult. In my time, Clive Lloyd was the statesman, and they got it right with a stream of brilliant cricketers. They also had a period where all their cricketers—guys like Joel Garner, Viv Richards, Malcolm Marshall, Courtney Walsh, Gordon Greenidge— were going into England, either playing league cricket or county cricket, and improving their skills. You learn how to play the game professionally in that environment, but it doesn't happen now, and they've declined at Test level as a result. I hope they can succeed in Twenty20 cricket and that it will cross over to the longer forms, because I'd like to see them strong again.

8

The pathway

THE GAME KEEPS moving forward. It's much more professional now than when I played, and we're extracting from the ranks fitter, stronger athletes who are better prepared, young guys who are learning better coping mechanisms to deal with the game.

Cricket Australia recently made arrangements to import pitch soil from India to lay down at the NCC in Brisbane for practice by the young players, and by our national team as well. They want our best players to experience subcontinental-style conditions for batting, in particular, and this is the best way to simulate it. 'If we can have a pitch here [in Australia] that really mirrors that, or pitches—three or four pitches that mirror an Indian, a Sri Lankan, Pakistan background if you like—that makes it easier to have the guys come up [to Brisbane] before a tour, rather than go to the tour earlier, and try and cram it,' said Darren Lehmann. 'You've got a lot more time to prepare which will, in essence, make them better players when they come under those conditions.' Needless to say, being beaten 4–0 against good spinners in India in 2013 has made this an imperative. The Australian team under Michael Clarke has a series against Pakistan in the United Arab Emirates in October 2014, where the wickets are spin-friendly and very different from what players experience here. Then there are Test match tours of Bangladesh, India and Sri Lanka over the next three years.

The issue is that our players are always vulnerable on spinning decks, and the results in India tell the tale. Australia has lost the last three series in India, in 2013, 2011 and 2009, following the drought-breaking 2004 series when Australia won for the first time in India for 35 years. 'One of the great challenges is winning away and that's why we're trying to get our guys used to playing in different conditions,' said Pat Howard, Cricket Australia's team performance manager. 'The subcontinent [pitch] idea has been around for a long time and we're very much trying to make this [National Cricket Centre] a place where in the middle of winter guys can get themselves ready and prepared.'

There's no doubt that we're vulnerable in this area at the moment. When I was in India in 2013 working in television, the wickets were very tough to play on, at least for an Australian. Our batsmen didn't handle it well, and the results reflected that. I feel that in the future, Australian teams will confront spinning wickets whenever they travel overseas unless we can do two things: prepare our batsmen better, and develop good spinners ourselves. Nathan Lyon's record as an off-spinner is very good, and people need to understand that none of the great offies from overseas have thrived on Australian wickets.

Lyon can be a very good spinner, while the likes of James Muirhead (Victoria), Cameron Boyce (Queensland), Ashton Agar (Western Australia) and Adam Zampa (South Australia) are all showing encouraging signs. We have quite a nice crop of slow bowlers at the moment, and we're going to need them. Just don't expect them to be Shane Warne, because that's the problem with Australian spinners. The expectations are crushing them.

Often now when a guy plays a less than judicious shot, he'll say, 'That's the way I play.' I suppose you can't criticise someone who's been told to play like that, such as a David Warner, but in a Test match I'd say, 'David, you still have to look at the bowlers and the conditions and the circumstances and be smarter in the way you play.' I must say, Warner has done this fantastically well, and he's improved a lot. Some guys can't stop the adrenalin rush; the smarter cricketers will cope, but it's a fine line. A guy like Michael Slater lived by the sword, died by the sword, and he was good enough for that to work. Some guys are naturally gifted and they have the smarts necessary to separate themselves from the pack. It's about how you apply your skills under pressure and ramp up your game or pull it back when required.

At the NCC in Brisbane, the young men play on different types of surfaces: slower, faster and bouncier. They have a bowling machine that actually simulates an opponent coming at them, via a video screen on the wall, so they can have Dale Steyn, for instance, steaming in and at the point of delivery the ball will come flying out of the wall exactly where the bowler would release it. It's a brilliant coaching tool, much better than the old bowling machines where you manually popped a ball into a rotating wheel that fired them out. With the current technology, a batsman can get the feel of playing in the middle and work on his trigger points to get his feet moving.

The NCC cost $29 million to set up, and it includes biomechanical force plates and an advanced motion-analysis camera system, a rehabilitation centre with a 25-metre lap pool and hot and cold plunge pools, medical consulting rooms, a gym and an Anti-Gravity Treadmill for rehabilitating injured players. Will it create better players? You'd like to think so and I certainly hope so. But it all begs the question about a country like Pakistan, whose performances are incredible. The way they can produce competitive cricket teams with all the dramas around their side and their country is freakish.

The pathway

Following the 2009 terrorist attack on the Sri Lankan team bus in Lahore, the ICC has stopped scheduling international cricket in Pakistan. In Pakistan, you can't play cricket up in Quetta or Peshawar because the Taliban won't have it, and the nation can't host a visiting country even in the main centres. On top of all this, Pakistan has had players suspended for spot-fixing. And yet they always manage to produce a competitive cricket team when there's no way they have anything approaching the structures we have in Australia.

What it shows, I guess, is that we're talking only percentage increments of difference. When push comes to shove, we're usually the No. 1 or No. 2 team in both Tests and one-day internationals, while Pakistan hasn't been No. 1 for a while. If our structure in Australia were the same as 50 years ago, we'd still produce a good cricket team, but we might be consistently ranked third or fourth in the world. To get past the teams ranked first, second or third, for instance, you have to be fitter, stronger, better prepared rather than simply talented.

The way we're set up with the NCC, coaching and domestic competitions, in particular the Sheffield Shield, Australia *ought* to be good. We should never drop off too much when you compare our system with what's available to cricketers in the West Indies and Pakistan, or even in New Zealand, where rugby union is far more popular. England, like us, has no excuses because their system is good, and

India isn't short of cash. What isn't clear is how much of the money floating around in Indian cricket actually filters through to infrastructure and the preparation of players, but then again, the Indians have the weight of numbers. They have a billion people and it seems they're all cricket crazy. But in Australia we should never be ranked as low as fifth, which is precisely where we'd slid in the world Test rankings in 2011, around the time the Argus report was being prepared. Something is definitely wrong if Australia slumps that low.

My PATHWAY TO playing for Australia was somewhat different from that a young man would experience now. I grew up with my parents and three brothers in Mosman, on the north shore of Sydney Harbour. Dad was a wool classer, Mum ran a delicatessen, and we lived in a Federation-style house directly across the road from Mosman oval. I spent my youth playing cricket and baseball at that ground, as well as in the backyard with my three brothers. My eldest brother, Mark, gave me my first pair of batting gloves.

Dad was a country slogger as a player; I can remember seeing him play a game for Ramsgate RSL in the St George area, and the slog to 'cow corner' was his shot of preference. He was right-handed and, oddly, I'm the only left-hander among my immediate family. My brothers are all very right-handed and my four children are all very right-handed. Mum did say that she started off writing left-handed in her early days but was persuaded to change, as they tended to be back then. I actually write or chop with an axe or shoot a pistol or use a screwdriver or eat with a spoon right-handed, but I kick a ball left-footed. I'm left-eye dominant, which must be a throwback to another generation.

I WENT TO school at Mosman Primary with Rob Hirst, who became the drummer for the rock band Midnight Oil, and Tom Burlinson, the actor/entertainer. In 1967 all three of us were prefects. I've run into Rob a couple of times, including once at Noosa Heads a few years ago. We've followed each other's careers.

In the early days there was always cricket or baseball happening at the oval, cricket in summer and baseball in winter. I was playing baseball at six, even earlier than I started cricket, and I loved the game. But I did gravitate to Mosman's junior cricket team, and I made my first century at Cammeray in the under-12s. I can remember Dad driving over to the shop and persuading Mum to close it for a while so they could come back to the ground and see me reach the ton.

Baseball helped my cricket, I've no doubt. The two sports complement each other well, particularly moving to the ball, picking up and throwing accurately. I started life in baseball as a pitcher, where I needed to throw accurately and I learnt to hit targets, which came through later in cricket. It was handy for me, particularly when one-day cricket became more prevalent and I was fielding at that mid-wicket slot.

I played baseball and cricket until I was about 17, and then baseball changed from a winter to a summer sport. I think they had grand plans of taking on cricket because the football codes were entrenched, or maybe they were coming into line with the American season. I tried to play both for a period around 17 or 18—cricket on Saturday, baseball on Sunday—and I loved it. I didn't find changing from one to the other any great challenge.

The cricket started to happen for me around that time, and when I began to play in representative sides it was hard to maintain both, so I concentrated more on cricket. I can remember listening to the Ashes tour, either in 1964 or 1968 when Doug Walters and Bob Simpson were there, on an old crystal radio set at home. My first cricket bat was a Bob Simpson autograph, so it was nice when I ended up playing with Simmo and having him as national coach when I was captain.

I can remember going to the SCG and watching from the old Hill in the late sixties and early seventies, seeing the South African Barry Richards get a big hundred for South Australia against New South Wales in 1970–71, and I recall my interest being piqued during the 1972 Ashes tour of England, when there were highlights on television every night. The fast bowler David Colley was on that touring team and he came from Mosman, so there was a direct interest there for me, because by that time I was playing the odd game in first grade.

My earliest hero would have been Garry Sobers, the West Indian all-rounder and all-time great. Mosman Cricket Club had a super-eight reel of the tied Test at Brisbane in 1960, which they showed at a film night at the council chambers when I was a kid. I liked the fact that Sobers was left-handed and a bit flamboyant.

I WASN'T THE world's best student. I started at North Sydney Technical High School, but it was sold for development, so I moved to North Sydney Boys High School in Falcon Street. My failure to fully focus is the reason I've driven my own children a little harder. I spent far too much time over in St Leonards Park, dreaming, but I did go to sixth form (Year 12), although I never went to university. If I had my time again, I'd probably try to get a trade certificate.

Junior cricket was a great education for me, because I was always playing against older boys. We played on mats a lot, which meant we learnt how to duck and weave, and there'd always be a bit of chirp out on the field. The ball flew off those wickets, and it was the right place to learn how to hook and cut. We also played a bit on malthoid, a synthetic wicket and a good learning surface, in my opinion, far better for kids than a turf wicket. I've always thought young cricketers should stick to playing on synthetic strips until they're 12 or 13, so they learn to play with consistent bounce.

My earliest coach was Tom Fleming, a good man who was strict with his discipline. He had a stiff knee from a motorbike accident, but he'd chase us around and clip us around the ear if we were mucking up. We learnt how to pack the kit properly, put the stumps in at the right height, that sort of thing, because he was a stickler for preparation. I learnt by observation in those days, and we'd stand in a circle hitting catches, the same kind of drills that are done today.

Tom was a strong bloke to have around, and my father John was always watching or umpiring or involved in some way. I had good support from my parents. Dad never said too much, but as my cricket developed, he used to sit on the front steps of our house with a cigarette, watching the cricket over the road. I'd get caught behind and come home and he'd say, 'I see you're still flashing outside off stump.' That was about the extent of the conversation. He was never telling me, 'Keep your left elbow up,' or, 'Get your right foot to the ball.'

I was picked for Mosman first grade at 16, and I dropped in and out of the team, but around that time my interests started to diverge and I was learning to drive.

The pathway

Going to Balmoral Beach seemed a lot more fun, and cricket became something I did on Saturdays rather than my be-all and end-all. At that point, I wasn't thinking, 'I'm going to play for Australia.' Quite early on, I played grade cricket against Bankstown, who had Jeff Thomson and Len Pascoe as their fearsome opening attack, and found out that Lenny had white-line fever. I also played a bit of representative cricket with Andrew Hilditch, who was making a lot of grade runs for Sutherland and starting to shine. Then Andrew was picked in the state squad, and I had one of those moments: 'If he can do it, maybe I can do it too.'

Barry Knight, a former England player, was captain–coach of Mosman, and it was Barry who really turned my career when it needed shaping. He was the catalyst for me having a proper crack at the game, improving my technique and generally trying to get better. Barry had set himself up as a professional coach, the first in Australia, after emigrating from England, where he played 29 Test matches as an all-rounder. He invited me down to practise at his cricket centre in Kent Street, in the city. I had the basics, but I needed to hit a lot more balls with those old whirligig bowling machines that were such a nightmare to encounter. They had a sudden release of the ball and at times they wouldn't fire the balls out properly, which meant you might suddenly cop the world's best bouncer. Of course the modern machines spit the balls out quite evenly.

I went down to the city a couple of nights a week for five weeks, and then Dad agreed to pay for more lessons because he could see it was working for me. Barry tightened me up, because when I was young I wanted to hit every second ball to the boundary. I worked on defence, building an innings, psychological things you don't think about when you're young. I'd started out as a 'see it, hit it' player, just whacking the ball, but soon enough I was learning the value of accumulating ones and twos, the whole process of batting and the smarts required. I made some minor adjustments, getting my foot to the ball and the traditional things coaches talk about. The 'see it, hit it' thing was still there, but I started doing it better.

Barry was ahead of his time with the video he'd set up, and it was a first for me. Even today, I think it's a great coaching tool. With all the data that's collected now, the best stuff is still old-fashioned video where you can watch yourself bat, and of course you need someone who knows your game well to help you. Barry Knight came to know my game and he had a significant impact on my career. I was still enjoying my baseball, but he said, 'You're good enough to play for your country. Do you know what that means? It means the world is yours. Baseball can't offer you that. You might get a game against the "also-rans" from Japan and America, but you'll never get a game against any "all-stars". In cricket, you will.'

•

In February 1993 I passed the world record for the most Test runs scored with this sweep shot for four in the First Test against NZ in Christchurch. I was keen to get the distraction out of the way.

(Joe Mann/Allsport UK/Getty Images)

Mike Gatting's other favourite moment in cricket was when he was bowled for four by Shane Warne with the first ball Warnie bowled in the First Test match in the 1993 Ashes at Old Trafford in Manchester. We had a new secret weapon, but even we were astounded by 'that ball'.

(David Munden/Popperfoto/Getty Images)

We went on to win the First Test and Warnie took 34 wickets in the series. It was a win worth celebrating. (David Munden/Popperfoto/Getty Images)

By the end of the Fourth Test at Headingley we had retained the Ashes. Graham Gooch is applauding Steve Waugh (157*) and me (200*) as we walk off the ground exhausted. We declared at 653 and won the match by an innings and 148 runs. (David Munden/Popperfoto/Getty Images)

Danny Morrison and I are good mates, but on this occasion after getting me out we exchanged a few pleasantries. (Ben Radford/Allsport/Getty Images)

My last Test match for Australia was the Third Test between South Africa and Australia in March 1994 at Kingsmead, in Durban, South Africa. It's hard to believe 20 years have passed since then. (Getty Images)

One of the biggest controversies that has dogged the sport over many decades is throwing. In 1995 at the Boxing Day Test at the MCG, Australian umpire Darrell Hair no-balled Muttiah Muralitharan of Sri Lanka seven times. (Vivian Jenkins/Getty Images)

Darren Lehmann took over as coach of the Australian side in 2013. He believes in a mix of old-fashioned values and a fair bit of fun. It's been good for the players. (Hamish Blair/ Allsport/Getty Images)

I'm not a fan of hanging around waiting for the third umpire's decision. The game needs to keep ticking over, and Test cricket needs to make sure there aren't so many breaks for drinks, injury treatment and referrals or we'll lose the audience. (Jack Atley/Allsport/Getty Images)

During the one-day series in India in 2007, Andrew Symonds was racially abused by the crowds at a couple of matches and then allegedly abused by Harbhajan Singh in Mumbai. This was the start of 'Monkeygate'. (Hamish Blair/Getty Images)

The non-stop action of the Big Bash makes the matches fun to watch. The Sydney Sixers and the Brisbane Heat are fierce competitors, and I'd like more top players to get involved. (Mark Metcalfe/Getty Images)

The rise of Twenty20 and the IPL has changed the game enormously. Some of Australia's most charismatic players and biggest hitters are huge stars of the IPL. Here Michael Hussey of the Chennai Super Kings sweeps while Adam Gilchrist of the Deccan Chargers looks on during a 2010 match in Nagpur, India. (Hamish Blair/IPL/Getty Images)

David Warner is a fan of switch-hitting, where he swaps from his natural left hand to his right hand for maximum effect. It's innovative but I'm not sure it's fair to the bowler. (Matt King/Stringer/Getty Images)

The Netherlands competed in the ICC Twenty20 World Cup in Bangladesh in 2014 and ranked ninth out of sixteen teams. I'm hoping we continue to see more development of some of the minor teams over the next few years. (Pal Pillai-IDI/IPL/ Getty Images)

Walking the Kokoda Track with my eldest, Dene, for his 21st birthday and Anzac Day, was tough but a great bonding experience. Not so much for the caterpillars.

Needless to say, my family—Dene, Jane, Nicole, Tara and Lachlan—are the most important people in the world to me.

The pathway

ONE OF THE best trips a young cricketer can make is to England. I went twice in my youth, the first time to Gloucestershire in 1977, when I played some second XI cricket and had a ball playing at Downend, where Dr W.G. Grace, the famous English player from days of yore, had his medical practice. I'd quit my clerical job at the BP film library in Sydney so I could travel there, even though it wasn't professional cricket. I'd also made my debut for New South Wales at Sheffield Shield level by that time, and it was the year the great WSC split was announced.

I watched the split from a distance, not really knowing at the time that it would open doors for me. I came back from Gloucestershire, played another season for New South Wales and then signed to play as a professional with East Lancashire in the Lancashire League in 1978. While I was there, Peter Spence, the New South Wales coach, sent me a questionnaire. One of the categories was 'Occupation'. I thought about it and wrote, 'Professional cricketer'. It was the first time I'd even thought like that, but England had helped me, particularly the experience on the different tracks and the notion that I had to perform.

As the pro at East Lancashire, certain things were expected of me. To begin with, I was the main man in the team, which was a new experience for me. I was expected to bowl the opposition out, get all the runs and take all the catches! It was fun, and it taught me that professionalism of grinding out a score if I had to, or taking some wickets—although I was somewhat of a failure in that respect. We had a wizened older guy bowling leg-spinners, and every time someone tonked a ball up in the air they'd all yell out, 'Pro!' and I'd have to run from long-on and try to take the catch, wherever it was landing. It was all great fun.

Before then I'd pumped petrol and worked at BP to pay the bills, taking leave so that I could go and play on the southern tour for New South Wales. A lot of guys were the same in those days, taking leave from their jobs when it was required and disappearing from work at four o'clock to make it for practice, making up the lost time on a Monday. A lot of them would work for sponsors involved with the cricket. I myself had my mind made up for me. I enjoyed playing for a living in Lancashire, and I was ensconced in the New South Wales team. I was picked to play for Australia for the first time in December 1978, against England at Melbourne, at the age of 23. The rest, as they say, is history.

9

Politics

I NEVER LIKED the politics in cricket, and a stint on Cricket Australia's board only reinforced my feelings. In particular, I still feel uncomfortable about the way our board handled the 'Monkeygate' controversy involving Andrew Symonds, who has West Indian heritage, and Harbhajan Singh of India in 2007–08.

After I retired, I felt I should put something back into the game, so I joined the board of Queensland Cricket after Peter Burge passed away in 2001. I enjoyed that for a period, and I'm still involved to this day. I became Queensland Cricket's delegate to the Cricket Australia board in 2002, replacing Cam Battersby. What I quickly found was that Queensland Cricket and Cricket Australia were two vastly different beasts, albeit governing the same game.

With Queensland, there was no real politics to speak of, no rivalries to deal with. Everyone was about doing the best for Queensland cricket. When I joined the national body, I found a lot more state parochial rhetoric around national decisions, which is probably to be expected, although it was frustrating.

At Queensland, every decision was pared back to this: 'How does it affect Queensland cricket?' At the national level, it was about 'Who gets the one-day game here?' and 'Who gets the Test match there?' or 'If I go back to my board with this decision, I might get the sack.' Generally speaking, matters would flow along and the management would write papers for board members to digest and vote on. Financials weren't my strong point, so I deferred to other people when it came to that. I was on the board for my cricket expertise, having a feel for the game and what the players might think. But I'm not a political animal.

Since my departure, Cricket Australia has been stream-lined, and more of that will happen gradually. Initially it will have a nine-man board of three 'independents' unaligned with the state associations, and six directors— one from each state. The changes to the Cricket Australia board structure have been very good.

THE ANDREW SYMONDS issue cropped up during and after the Sydney Test match against India in January 2008. It was a nasty match that Australia won narrowly, but there were some controversial umpiring decisions, particularly on the final day. There was a lot of angst on both sides, and it ended in a race scandal that threatened to split the cricket world and end the tour.

In hindsight, all the problems could be said to have begun during the world Twenty20 championship semi-final in Durban the previous year, when the Australian and Indian dugouts were placed side by side and there was banter going each way. India won that semi-final and went on to beat Pakistan in the final, but Symonds was quoted afterwards in a hint of what was to come: 'We have had a very successful side and I think watching how we celebrate and how they celebrate, I think we have been pretty humble in the way we have gone about it. Personally, I think they [India] have got far too carried away with their celebrations. It has definitely sparked passion inside of us.'

The tension built. There was a one-day series in India in September–October 2007, and Symonds, who was Man of the Series, was racially abused by the crowds in Vadodara and Nagpur and then allegedly by Harbhajan Singh in Mumbai. After the seventh international of that series, there was a meeting to arbitrate between Harbhajan and Symonds in which the Australians claimed Harbhajan had called Symonds a 'monkey'. The Australians left the meeting feeling that everyone had agreed the word was unacceptable; the Indians claimed later that the agreement was only to stop sledging each other. This point was important, because when Harbhajan and Symonds clashed in Sydney on day three of the New Year Test match, and Symonds believed he heard the Indian spinner call him 'monkey' again, he felt the Mumbai agreement had been broken.

After the Mumbai problem, the Board for Control of Cricket in India (BCCI) did nothing until the ICC pressured it to take action. In the end, the BCCI merely issued a joint statement with Cricket Australia condemning racism. The Australians felt the matter was over, but then in Sydney, Harbhajan, engaged in a furious battle with Brett Lee and, having slashed the Australian quick for a boundary, patted him on the backside with his bat as he trotted down the pitch, as if to say, 'Bad luck.' Harbhajan and Lee have a good relationship.

But Symonds saw the exchange differently, and he took offence. In his newspaper column of the time, Symonds said he believed he should back his teammate, Lee. 'I'm a firm believer in sticking up for your teammate, so I stepped in and had a bit of a crack at Harbhajan, telling him exactly what I thought of his antics,' he wrote. 'He then had a shot back, which brings us to the situation we're facing.' At the end of Lee's over, Harbhajan gestured for Symonds to come towards him. They walked a few steps together talking, although there was no outward sign of fury. Other players joined in, first Matthew Hayden, then Sachin Tendulkar, the non-striking batsman, then Ricky

Ponting, the Australian captain. Symonds claimed that Harbhajan called him a 'big monkey'; television footage of the exchange shows the Australian holding two fingers up to Harbhajan, indicating that this was the second time he'd been abused. Symonds was upset, and rightly so.

In the hearing that followed, Symonds, Hayden and Michael Clarke all said they'd heard Harbhajan Singh call Andrew Symonds a monkey, but the umpires didn't. Nothing was picked up through the stump microphones, and Harbhajan claimed he'd actually used the expression *teri ma ki chut*, a Hindi curse that translates as 'mother-fucker'. Both Harbhajan and Tendulkar claimed this had been misheard by Symonds and the Australians.

There was a huge amount of heat in the situation by the time ICC referee Mike Procter handed Harbhajan Singh a three-match suspension for racial abuse. The Indians felt slighted that their story wasn't accepted, and the team soon threatened to go home with two Tests remaining. Many Australians felt that India, 2–0 down in the series, were whingers. As tensions boiled between the two teams and the two countries, Harbhajan appealed, and the ICC brought in New Zealand High Court judge Justice John Hansen to hear the matter. Hansen threw out the racism part of the charge, and fined the spinner $3000, or 50 per cent of his match fee, for verbal abuse.

The downgrading of the charge enraged the Australian players, but Hansen criticised Symonds for misinterpreting the initial action by Harbhajan to Lee, the pat on the backside: 'Anyone observing this incident would take it to be a clear acknowledgement of "well bowled".' Justice Hansen also acknowledged that an error by the ICC had contributed to the relatively light penalty imposed upon Harbhajan; the governing body had failed to reveal to the judge that the Indian spinner had been suspended several times before, including for a 2001 incident in which he was found to have attempted to intimidate an umpire.

I WAS ON the Cricket Australia board at the time, and we ultimately accepted the ICC appeal finding and moved on, but it's never sat well with me. We hung Andrew Symonds out to dry and at the time I was annoyed about it. I thought, 'This isn't right. Obviously something happened out there.' We were encouraging—and the ICC was encouraging— players to report racial slurs and vilification on the field, but when it actually happened, it went nowhere. It got ugly. When the Indians started to flex their muscles and threatened to go home, our players were very aggrieved. They felt that if the situation had been reversed and any of them had called someone a monkey, they'd have been hammered. They also felt that the earlier agreement from the Indian tour had been broken.

I was torn. Initially I was all for backing our players, but then the reality hit from a business point of view.

We were told we'd have a massive financial hole if the Indians went home, and we couldn't afford it. Channel Nine as the broadcaster could sue us for not producing the days of cricket specified by the television-rights contract, and then we'd have to countersue India. India are all-powerful now, so we'd have had no chance. The realisation at board level was that we couldn't have India go home. But morally and ethically we should have called their bluff and hoped the global community would hold them to order, even though I don't think that would have happened.

Once we were aware of the commercial realities, we knew we had to back down a bit. Andrew Symonds was aggrieved, and it affected him deeply. His cricket suffered from then on, and I think that was the start of it. He had trouble coping with his notoriety as a cricketer. He wanted to go to the pub with the boys, have a few beers and not find himself pestered. He was such a big star in that period, and he had no peace. Ironically, he and Harbhajan later became IPL teammates for a while at Mumbai Indians, and I think they got along all right. Harbhajan knew how to push our buttons, that's for sure. We play a hard game, but when someone plays a hard game against us, we're inclined not to like it.

As for Symonds, he never let it go. 'I think Cricket Australia was intimidated by the Indian cricket board,' he told the cricinfo website some time later:

The thing, I think, that was grinding on me the most was the lying. Because the allegation was that this hadn't happened, and it had. Then the lies started, and then it became political. The captain [Ricky Ponting] was made to look like a fool, and that should have never happened, and the other players too. If truth, honesty and common sense had prevailed then there'd have been a punishment for the player. It would have been dealt with and it would have set a precedent for the future.

That incident also hastened my departure from the board a little. The backroom deals were done, and I was out of my depth. They made the commercial decision, not the ethical/moral decision. Would India have actually stayed or gone home if we'd stood up to them? If they'd gone home, we'd at least have had the moral high ground. We thought we had basic proof that we were right, that there'd been a slur, and the ICC should have got more involved. I believe 'Symo', who said he heard it, as well as Hayden, Clarke and Ricky, who also heard it, and they're not inclined to make things up. In Harbhajan's defence, I suppose there's a chance they actually misheard what he said. Ultimately, the commercial realities and the dollars involved overran everything.

•

Politics

WHEN I BECAME a national selector in 1998, four years after my retirement, I was talking to Bill Brown, the former Test batsman who'd also been a selector. I mentioned to him how difficult the state rivalries became for a national selector, and he said, 'A.B., that's been going on forever.' He told me the Victorian board member might say, 'Bill, you didn't do too good getting *your* guy in the side today.' It was all about getting as many of your own state's players into the team as possible. That's totally wrong, so wrong.

Traditionally, people have said that if Victoria, for instance, has no national selector, they'll have trouble getting players picked for Australia. As a selector, that's just so annoying to hear. I'm an Australian first and a Queenslander second. I'm trying to pick the best team I can for Australia. If we end up picking 11 Victorians or 11 New South Welshman, then so be it. There's always that undercurrent that state selectors will push certain players forward. The state coaches might say things like, 'Where were the national selectors? We didn't see them at our game. It's affecting our players' chances.' There was actually talk at one point that Cricket Australia might give financial incentives for states producing international players rather than winning Sheffield Shields. That should be the priority for the states, but in reality, the captains and coaches at state level can fall into that notion of trying to win first of all, which I can also relate to.

I've tried to get this thinking through in Queensland, with Darren Lehmann as coach and more recently with Stuart Law. I suggested, 'Your job isn't dependent on winning Shields and Ryobi Cups. That would be a by-product of producing players to put in front of national selectors who can play for Australia. That's your job.' You push that idea, but inevitably a guy also wants that success as a coach.

I HAD TWO stints on the national selection panel, from 1998 to 2005 and again in 2006. Quite frankly, most of the time we'd argue about one or two spots in the team, because Australia had a magnificent side. There were ten certainties in every game. Wicketkeeper? Gilchrist. Spin bowler? Warne. Fast bowler? McGrath. No. 3 batsman? Ponting. Openers? Hayden and Langer. It was hardly rocket science for us, and ultimately it might come down to whether we'd include a second spinner in the squad rather than another quick bowler.

Having said that, we did have a couple of tough calls, and those moments do indicate what a tricky job it is. Undoubtedly, the hardest in my time was the decision to cut Steve Waugh out of the one-day team in 2002, which removed the captaincy from him and made Ricky Ponting the one-day skipper. Steve had come through during my time as captain and grown into the wonderful player he was, but in the summer of 2001–02 Australia missed the finals of the triangular one-day competition, leaving South Africa and New Zealand to fight out the final. This was a rare event. More to the point, the World Cup in South Africa was only a year away and, as selectors, we wanted to work towards that.

Steve was 36, he wasn't bowling much because of back and shin problems, and he wasn't playing all that well— not to his usual high standard anyway; his place in the Test team was also under scrutiny. The one-day team was a worry for us. Soon after the finals of the triangular series, Trevor Hohns, the chairman of selectors, and I were in Melbourne for the Border Medal and met 'Tugga' in the team hotel. We'd decided to leave him out of the team that was about to tour Zimbabwe and South Africa for some one-day matches, and run with some youth, but we wanted to tell him face to face. I went along to support Trevor, who'd been required to deliver bad news to quite a few players as chairman. I knew it would be tough, given all three of us had been in the team that won back the Ashes in 1989 and we went way back.

It was just as tough as I expected. Steve didn't take it well, which I could understand, and said he thought he could still contribute to the team. It wasn't so much anger that came out, but logic and a bit of defiance. He was saying, 'I disagree, I don't think you're making the right decision here.' At that point he hadn't been left out of the

World Cup team, because that was a year away. But at his age, the implication was there. As it was such a momentous decision, Cricket Australia called a press conference in Melbourne on 13 February 2002 to announce it, and Trevor sat alongside Steve and James Sutherland, the chief executive, so that all could explain their positions.

Trevor Hohns is a straight-up guy and he put it bluntly: 'It was the selectors' unanimous view that there were now other players ahead of Steve for a place in the one-day team and now is the appropriate time to do some serious planning for the World Cup.'

Steve was typically philosophical: 'I'll definitely remain available for Australia for one-day cricket. I'd love to be part of the World Cup campaign in 2003. This I see as a setback and challenge. I've never shied away from a challenge. I'm a determined person and I'll do everything in my power to get back in that one-day side. My campaign starts from today.'

Asked how he felt at such a slight, Steve answered, 'There's no shame in being dropped from a side. I mean, we all give it our best shot. Occasionally, the performances aren't up to scratch and sometimes you get dropped. This is a setback. This isn't career-ending for me.'

More than a decade on it's easy for people to forget how much of a furore this one decision created in Australia. In an instant, the selectors became pariahs around the country. Many people were mortified at the treatment of an iconic figure like Steve Waugh, and most of the bile was directed at Trevor Hohns as the chairman. *The Daily Telegraph* in Sydney, one of the country's biggest-selling newspapers, published a front-page cartoon of the four selectors with dunces' hats on. At the time, I couldn't help but notice the irony of the situation, given the media had been criticising Steve over his form and debating his future. But when the hard call was made, the argument turned full circle.

It wasn't a pleasant time, particularly for Trevor, although he's a strong person and he worked through it. I had no problem with Steve saying he intended to make it impossible for the selectors to leave him out of the World Cup team. He went back to the New South Wales colours and he played well, too. The following summer, 2002–03, was an Ashes series, and Australia won 4–1 under Steve's captaincy, but there was now a bubbling debate about when he'd retire from Test cricket.

I'll never forget the day Steve peeled off a century in the Sydney Test match against England in January of that season, hitting a boundary from the last ball of the day bowled by off-spinner Richard Dawson. This was a euphoric day for both Steve and Australian cricket. He'd reached 10,000 Test runs and he'd seen off the wolves at his own door (it had been reported in the media that Trevor Hohns had met Steve before the Perth Test to discuss his future). 'At the moment Stephen has our support until the

Sydney [Fifth] Test,' Hohns was quoted as saying before the match. 'The decision is then up to him whether he wants to continue or not. If he does, he will be judged on form like any other player.'

Steve's Sydney performance came to tumultuous applause around the country. David Boon, who was also a selector, joined me in the dressing rooms after play and we congratulated Steve on his innings. Then Boonie and I went to find a taxi to our hotel. I suggested we wander down towards the old Sydney Showground to find a cab rank. That was a mistake. There was a packed bar area right next door to the taxi queue, and we were recognised and started copping heaps, some of it good natured but some of it vitriolic: 'You can't dump him now, you bastards!' We just kept our heads down, hoping for a taxi to turn up.

That's the selector's lot. Australians are passionate about the make-up of their cricket team, and for the people who actually do the selecting, it's a thankless task, a little like refereeing. You're in the firing line—you make one mistake and it's a media headline the next day. In that period we were winning Test matches hand over fist, but it was that decision that sparked debate.

Steve Waugh never played another one-day international, and he retired from Test cricket at the end of the following season, 2003–04. In his autobiography, *Out of My Comfort Zone*, Steve articulated his anger at the selection panel over his dumping from the one-day team:

I didn't have a problem with the decision. However, I did have an issue with the lack of man-management skills involved . . . Surely, after so many years playing and being the captain of a side that had been ranked No. 7 when I took over and was now No. 1, at least one phone call or conversation letting me know how the selectors saw the bigger picture would have been nice . . . The clinical efficiency of my dismissal stung me most, because as a player I had always given everything.

Steve Waugh is an iconic player and he'd also been a great one-day player for a long time. As a selector, I was thinking, 'Have I got the right to do this? Should he be allowed to call time on his own career?' I had a nauseous feeling when I walked out of that room after telling Steve he'd been dropped. In the end, we picked Andrew Symonds to play in the 2003 World Cup side. He wasn't in sparkling touch at the time, but we'd gone with him anyway. I can remember watching our first game. Australia was playing Pakistan and we were five for not-many, and I thought, 'Oh my God, how handy would it be to have Steve Waugh going in right now?' Then Symonds flogged 143 not out, we won the game, went on a roll and won the World Cup. As tough as that decision was, it was vindicated.

•

IAN HEALY'S DEPARTURE in 1999 was only marginally easier. I was away with the national team in Zimbabwe when Geoff Marsh, the coach, quit after a close friend died at home. I was left to coach the team for a short period and, at the time, 'Heals' was under pressure for his position. It wasn't so much that his wicketkeeping had slumped, but his batting was definitely in decline.

During that trip I had a conversation with Ian, who basically said, 'Look, I'm going to retire, but I'd like to play one more game.' The first Test of the summer was in Brisbane, and he wanted to play there before walking away. Heals was 35 and he'd enjoyed a stellar career, but the time had come. I told him it was okay by me, that the Gabba seemed a good place to finish given he was a Queenslander, but I did add that I'd need to speak to Trevor Hohns as chairman of selectors first.

When I contacted Trevor, he was very strongly against giving Ian a farewell Test match. He said, 'We can't have that. If we're going to have a new keeper, then it's got to be now.' What I didn't know was that Hohns had already talked to Healy earlier about his possible phasing-out. Trevor said to me, 'I told Ian that if we hadn't seen a marked improvement [in Zimbabwe] that we'd make a change.' That's why Trevor wasn't happy for Ian to play at the Gabba against Pakistan and then walk, one Test in to a series. And there was the matter of the kid called Gilchrist.

Adam Gilchrist had been the wicketkeeper for one-day cricket for three years already, and at 27 years old was screaming out to play Test cricket. 'Gilly' had played a big part in the 1999 World Cup triumph under Steve Waugh's captaincy, and he already had five one-day international hundreds to his name, while his keeping was improving.

Ian Healy played his last Test match for Australia in Harare, Zimbabwe, before a handful of spectators. He didn't take our decision well, and there's no doubt that the situation didn't play out ideally. But not every story has the fairytale ending, unfortunately. It affected the relationship between Trevor Hohns and Heals for a while, although I like to think they're okay now. When you're in the middle of it, as I was, you'll always think, 'Why couldn't it be done that way?' It was a tough one, but that's what selectors are there for.

SELECTORS WILL BE required to force players out more and more over time, but I don't blame the cricketers for holding on. They make a good living, they have a great lifestyle, and it's hard to let go when you're passionate about something. It's easy for a player to think, 'How can I get a job that matches this? If I can extract one more year, that's another potential million in my kick.'

The selectors need to make the hard calls when required, but it's getting harder. When cricket was purely amateur, or semi-professional, or even what it was like in my time, you just got dropped from a team and you generally deserved to go. Nowadays it's more akin to a workplace scenario, where an employee might need to be warned first. In the Olympic sports, for instance, people left out of a team can appeal to the Court of Arbitration for Sport (CAS) and plead their case. I can see this arising in cricket soon enough: 'So you've left Steve Waugh out, he's got 10,000 runs, he's averaging 50.' What would a selector say to that? He can't argue, 'He's 36, we want to refresh.'

I've heard that when David Boon retired, he went to his old mate, Geoff Marsh, and asked him whether he was guaranteed a spot in the team. Marsh was coaching Australia at the time, and he couldn't provide the guarantee. Boonie walked away on that honest assessment, completing a fabulous career. I think his retirement was handled really well.

A veteran player will often have a 'light-bulb' moment when he knows he's finished. In Ricky Ponting's last season, for example, against South Africa in the summer of 2012–13, he'd been pondering retirement and his numbers were diminishing. Then Jacques Kallis bowled him with a wicked away-swinger in the Adelaide Test, and Ricky ended up losing his balance and falling on the deck, with his castle disturbed. He's said that this was the catalyst for his decision to retire. Within a few days, he'd announced that the next Test match, in Perth, would be his last.

But I never had that moment. As I moved into the latter part of my career, I'd ask past players about the right time to go. Ian Chappell said, 'You'll just wake up and know, A.B.' Not in my case. I guess I figured I might make five ducks in a row, or completely lose my mojo as a batsman and have the decision made for me. But the truth is that in that 1993–94 period when everyone was debating when I might retire from international cricket, I was enjoying getting out of bed each day to go and play.

When I finally did retire from international cricket, at the end of the 1994 South African tour, it was overdue. In fact, I'll openly admit now that I played 12 months too long. But I was still enjoying the game and I'd never toured South Africa. They'd just been readmitted to international cricket and it would be our first official tour there since the late sixties, so there was some history attached to it.

I'd started to become a bit annoyed by people asking me through that period around 1993, 'When are you going to retire?' I didn't have the answer. Although I could tell myself that I wasn't playing with anywhere near as much freedom—some of my go-to shots weren't happening and scoring runs was a lot harder—I hadn't really dropped off that badly. I'd made a double century at Leeds on the Ashes tour, and we were playing some outstanding cricket. By this time we'd won three consecutive Ashes series and we came terribly close to beating the West Indies in the home summer of 1992–93, one of the big disappointments of my career.

From the end of September 1988 to August 1992 I didn't get a hundred in a Test, but then I made another four in the next two years, including that double ton in England. Sometimes I found myself thinking, 'Maybe it's time,' but I always liked practising, going to the nets, trying to maintain a level or trying to get better. It wasn't like my eyes went or my knees went and I wasn't moving well. Mentally I felt sharp. I never had an issue about loving to go out there to play, and it got harder and harder to say, 'This is the time,' because I was enjoying it.

I should have finished after the 1993 Ashes tour. I didn't play terribly, but my powers were waning when we played South Africa at home, and my range of shots against their bowling on our tracks was limited. When we went to South Africa, I knew that was it, but my stubbornness kept me from saying anything. I was so sick and tired of getting asked every day that I just thought, 'You know what? I won't say anything.' But inwardly I knew this was going to be it.

I might have told Austin Robertson, my manager at the time, that I was thinking about it, and possibly my wife Jane, and I had a benefit year in Australia in 1993–94, which signalled to everyone that it was close. In hindsight, I should have made an announcement, but I didn't particularly want any fanfare. I just wanted to finish. Then, of course, the stubbornness kicked in.

In the end, I handled it poorly. My last Test, in March 1994, was a boring draw in Durban and I was very disappointed with the way the South Africans played. They'd bowled us out for 269 in the first innings, but they didn't force the issue, even though the series was tied at 1–1. They scored at just over two runs an over, so by the time we batted again, we had no option but to play for a draw. Still, when I walked out to bat in the second dig at 4–157, we'd only just overtaken their first-innings lead. I decided, 'If they're going to play like that, I'll play like that too.' It was one of the dullest Test matches I've ever played in. I got 42 not out in nearly four hours on the last day.

I still hadn't told any of the players I was retiring, but I should have done. I could have announced it before the tour, or maybe even not gone on that tour. Eventually I told Jane, and when I came home after a few one-dayers in South Africa, I rang Laurie Sawle, the chairman of selectors, and told him I was going to quit. I said, 'It's time. I'm going to announce my retirement.' But to my surprise, Laurie said, 'Can you hold off? Because if you tell the board now, it'll leak. We just want to put things in place so it's all done properly.'

A week or two went by and I hadn't heard anything from the board. I kept it to myself, and nothing was happening. Then on the news one night it was reported that the board had called in David Boon and Mark Taylor (among other senior players) to discuss the leadership succession. The report said the board wanted to wait and see what I was doing, which was confusing and made me angry, given I'd already told Laurie Sawle. The next day, I went off to Brisbane to play golf with my friend Pat Welsh, the Channel Seven sports presenter and reporter, and told him what was happening. That night I went on the news with Paddy and gave him the big scoop.

That didn't go over well, either. The board was annoyed with me—quite rightly, I suppose—because they'd wanted to make some sort of fuss about the announcement. Kerry Packer wasn't enamoured of me either, because he'd been good to me through my benefit year. It was my fault. Even at the testimonial dinner the season before I could have made an announcement. I'd had ample opportunity but I never really felt like I wanted to give it away.

There's no doubt that it would have been nice to have done it better. I didn't want a huge fanfare, but it could have been more appropriate. In the end, it was announced, Mark Taylor was appointed as the new captain, and I went back to play for Queensland in the quest for that elusive Sheffield Shield, to break the curse that had gripped the state since the inception of the competition in the twenties.

But the finish to my international career is a regret that burns. I know I should have done it better, but you can't always have the fairytale ending. The fairy tale was the career.

WE WENT THROUGH a phase immediately after my retirement and right through until recently when our second team could have been very competitive in Test cricket. Players like Darren Lehmann, Stuart Law and Jamie Siddons were great batsmen who should have played a lot of Test cricket. Lehmann should have been a 100-Test player but only played 27. Darren Berry was Victoria's keeper and the best in the land for a long time, but never played a Test match.

Dean Jones never played Test cricket after the tour of Sri Lanka in 1992 and he had a 46.55 average. Imagine leaving out a player with those numbers in recent years; a 46 average would see you the first picked! If we'd picked a second Test team around the time I coached the Australia A, not long after I retired, then we'd arguably have been No. 2 in the world, with Matthew Hayden, Damien Martyn, Greg Blewett and the others. We took Hayden and Martyn on the 1993 Ashes tour and they didn't get a single Test match, yet they both made 1000 runs for the season. That's how tough it was to break in.

PERHAPS THE BIGGEST drama in my playing days regarding selection turned out to be a plus for us, in the selection of Peter Taylor for the last Test match of the 1986–87 Ashes series. We'd hit the low of lows in Melbourne, losing in three days, and the selectors came up with Peter, the New South Wales off-spinner, to play the last Test match at Sydney.

Hardly anyone knew Peter, which led to the infamous 'Peter Who?' headline. But I did know him; we'd played schoolboys together for New South Wales. When he was named in the team, the media speculated that there'd been an error, that the player picked was meant to be Mark Taylor, who at that point hadn't played for Australia. I gather one radio station in Sydney even rang Mark Taylor, who'd made his way into the New South Wales team at the time, and congratulated him on his national selection.

The selectors dined out on the fact that Peter Taylor came in and took eight wickets on an SCG turner—and we won the match, of course—but I do believe there was something wrong with that selection, because I was presented with a team that didn't have a second opening batsman beyond Geoff Marsh. David Boon had already been dropped. I can still remember sitting in the rooms and calling for a volunteer to open the batting with Swampy in that match, and Greg Ritchie was the man who put his hand up. But Ritchie wasn't an opening batsman; to my knowledge he'd never opened the batting before, and he wasn't opening in state cricket for Queensland.

The team wasn't balanced, and I maintain that the selectors either got the wrong Taylor, or that they meant to pick both Peter and Mark Taylor so as to have an opening batsman there, too. It mystified me then and it still does. No one came to me and said, 'This is the side. Greg Ritchie's going to open,' because in those days I wasn't consulted on selection. Thankfully, it worked out.

●

I WAS THE selector on duty in Hobart in 1999 when Scott Muller, the Queensland fast bowler, had to be told he'd been dropped. That came at the time of the infamous 'Can't bowl, can't throw' controversy. Muller had delivered a poor throw-in from the outfield during the Test match against Pakistan, and a mysterious voice came across the television coverage: 'Can't bowl, can't throw.'

I can 100 per cent guarantee that it wasn't Shane Warne who made that particular comment, but it was broadcast, the media picked up on it, and it became a very big story because it supposedly involved Warne. The theory was that Warnie was bowling at the time, and that his voice had been picked up through the stump microphones. In certain parts of the media this was considered sacrilege. How could an Australian player abuse a teammate in that way? Not only that, but Channel Nine's denials pushed the media into a conspiratorial tone. I went to Warnie about it, and he said, 'I'm a big enough man. If it was me, I'd own up to it. But it wasn't me, so I'm not owning up to something I didn't do.' He's actually told me that on numerous occasions, and I believe him.

The words were actually spoken by Joe Previtera, a long-time Channel Nine cameraman who was filming from the boundary near a boom-effects microphone, and that throwaway line was accidentally broadcast. The sound came through umpire Peter Parker's radio microphone and, because Parker was standing next to Warnie, he thought Shane had said it. Then Muller got the shits because he also believed it was Shane.

After all that, the selection panel left Muller out of the team for the next Test and I had to deliver the news. He didn't take it well and I can remember saying, 'It's not that you've done anything wrong, but . . .' A little while on, Scott went back to play a Shield or one-day game and after he got a wicket he yelled into the stump mike, 'What about that, Warnie?' It affected Scott. The media attention was enormous and he struggled with it. His own cricket started to fall away, and that was the last of his two Test matches for Australia. As for the kerfuffle, that's the Shane Warne effect. He polarises people, and just about anything he does (or doesn't do) is big news. This one just got way out of hand.

IN THOSE DAYS, of course, you weren't talking about million-dollar salaries as you are now. Try telling a player in the modern era he's going from a $2 million national contract down to a state-level contract. It's a huge decision, and the process is quite different. When the players have their post-season reviews, the selectors have to be careful what they say to the players. It's like a business, and you have to give some notice if you're about to move someone on.

Rod Marsh will do well as the new chairman of selectors, and Mark Waugh will be good because of his left-field thinking. He knows his cricketers and he has strong views on who can and can't play. His portfolio will be more the one-dayers and Twenty20, and Mark won't just toe the line or be a yes-man for anyone. Mark's more astute, hard-nosed and savvy than people realise. There's a lot to him.

In the future, it's bound to be difficult getting people of his quality to act as a selector, because they earn hardly anything in that job. It's just fortunate that Mark has television commitments that take him around to games anyway. Any of the quality people who retire from playing the game are more likely to move into the commercial world or into coaching. It will be guys like Trevor Hohns, who has run a business and then stepped back from that, who take these selection jobs.

But Australia has been fortunate. The 'Colonel', Laurie Sawle, was Australia's chairman of selectors for a lot of my playing days, and he was outstanding. Sawle, who'd played for Western Australia, was astute and he could make hard calls. The same could be said for Hohns.

CRICKET HAS BEEN ripped apart by match-fixing and illegal gambling interests since I retired, and it was only an undercurrent when I played. When I played one-day tournaments in Sharjah in the eighties, I heard that people were gambling on the toss, and of course Ladbrokes in England had been running odds on cricket for years. But when the illegal Indian bookmakers became interested in cricket, everything changed.

It saddens me the way the gambling interests have infiltrated the game in the last 20 years. As it happened, it was the year after I retired that Salim Malik as captain of Pakistan was alleged to have approached Shane Warne and Tim May in Lahore and offered them money to underperform on the final day of a Test match against Australia. Several other captains of Test nations have gone down: Hansie Cronje of South Africa and Mohammad Azharuddin of India, whom I played against, and more recently Salman Butt of Pakistan.

I was incredulous about Cronje, who was banned for life and who later died in an aeroplane accident. I just couldn't believe it. I thought, 'This is a smoke screen. They're blaming the good guy to protect someone else.' I thought he was the straightest shooter. There was no prouder South African, and he was quite a religious guy, with strong family ties and everything to gain from being who he was, the captain of South Africa. The style of bloke he was, he would have been financially fine forever. But I hadn't seen the other side of him, with that totally ruthless, relentless pursuit of the dollar.

Azharuddin I wouldn't have picked as being involved, either. I was once having a whinge to 'Azza' about captaincy and its pressures, and he said, 'Allan, you try being a Muslim and captaining India. That's pressure.' He had a point, although I wouldn't have picked him as a match-fixer in a million years. You can never be sure, can you? Once that hook goes in, how far can you be dragged? And we don't know what pressures have been brought to bear once a player goes down that path.

More recently, the advent of spread-betting and spot-betting (or spot-fixing) has changed the ball game substantially in the sense that a punter might bet on, say, the number of no-balls or when a wide would be bowled. I believe the players who've been caught up in these matters can more easily justify this behaviour to themselves and their conscience can deal with it, because they can argue that they're not actually *match-fixing*: 'I'm still trying to win the match. If I pick up some extra cash along the way because I bowl a no-ball off the third ball of the third over, then so be it.' Pakistan fast bowler Mohammad Amir is on suspension for bowling no-balls at a particular time after a British newspaper performed a sting in 2010, paying someone to act as an intermediary for a bookmaker. Amir was only 19, he came from a small village, he wasn't worldly and he alleges his captain was putting pressure on him. I do feel some sympathy for him.

The ICC has no judicial powers to deal with this stuff, and that's the problem. In the case of Cronje and the South African players who went down with him, they were caught accidentally by the Indian police when their names came up in a phone-tapping operation aimed at catching someone else. It's not as though the ICC is the FBI. It's just so hard to police without powers to subpoena witnesses and seize bank records.

In Australia, our players are very well paid, and that's a relief, because where's the temptation for them to get involved with bookmakers? They're already making good money, and they risk losing all that and more if they do something wrong. So we need to keep educating players about the rights and wrongs, and we need to ensure that in the global pie of money for cricket, the players are well rewarded. We also need judicial powers, and the threat of jail for players who cross the line, rather than mere suspensions. Cricket needs the big stick, because what's the threat now? A player can get banned, but he might set himself up for life if he can get away with it for a couple of years. Mind you, the three Pakistanis recently caught doing the wrong thing did spend time behind bars.

I WAS A young buck when the underarm controversy happened in 1981, in a one-day international between Australia and New Zealand at the MCG. The final act was that Trevor Chappell, under instruction from his elder brother Greg as Australian captain, bowled the last ball of New Zealand's 50 overs along the ground, with the Kiwis needing six runs to tie the match. But the controversy was only beginning at that point.

Politics

It had already been a controversial day, because in the Australian innings, Greg Chappell had been given not out after he hit an outfield shot to Martin Snedden, the New Zealand seamer, who appeared to catch it low down, sliding forward. Greg refused to walk because he wasn't convinced the ball had carried, while the Kiwis took umbrage since Snedden believed he'd taken it 'clean'. So the visitors were already seething when Australia won the match on that last delivery.

I'd been fielding in the deep when Trevor bowled the last over and I couldn't quite grasp what they were planning. I could see Greg and Trevor chatting, and Rod Marsh shaking his head as if to say, 'No way.' In those days, there were no boundary ropes and there weren't so many sixes hit, especially at the MCG with its vast boundaries. Brian McKechnie, New Zealand's No. 10, needed to clear the fence to tie the match. The odds against him would have been astronomical, so Greg's decision was a bit bizarre, to say the least.

McKechnie blocked the ball and threw away his bat in disgust, and I remember the crowd booing. It wasn't a good feeling at all, skulking up through the spectators and hearing the Kiwis giving us heaps from the open door of their dressing room as we filed past. I was young and I didn't say a thing. It was deathly quiet in the rooms afterwards. We'd won the game, but there was no celebration.

Greg had made a mistake. He was tired, not just from making a score earlier in the day, but from the grind of the summer and the captaincy. It was a snap decision and a stupid mistake, and he knows and acknowledges that. He talked about a WSC match in 1978, when the West Indian Wayne Daniel hit a six off the second-last ball to beat Australia, and the players had talked about preventing that scenario in the future. The answer they came up with was to bowl an underarm ball, although no one would have thought it a real possibility at the time, even though it was legal.

We sat quietly for what seemed an eternity in the old dressing rooms until Sam Loxton, the Test selector and cricket legend, came barging into the upstairs viewing room and yelled out, 'Well, you might have won the game, but you've lost a lot of friends.' Sam was very emotional, almost crying, and Dennis Lillee yelled back at him, 'Get fucked, Sam.' The ice was instantly broken and everyone started talking about the rights and wrongs of what had just happened.

There was a groundswell of negativity afterwards, and the New Zealand prime minister, Robert Muldoon, called it 'the most disgusting incident I can recall in the history of cricket', and passed some comment about our playing attire: 'I consider it appropriate that the Australian team were wearing yellow.' Greg copped it from all around, including the local commentators. Richie Benaud called it 'disgraceful' and 'one of the worst things I've ever seen done on a cricket field'.

Late that night, after a great deal of the amber fluid, Doug Walters made a bold claim: 'I could hit an underarm for six!' We said, 'Bullshit, Freddy, it's not possible.' He explained, 'You run down the wicket, flick it up with your front foot, and hit it over mid-wicket for six!' The funny thing is, when we were in Sydney for the next final, we coaxed Dougie into the nets so we could bowl underarm to him. He tried out his theory, and we were saying he was out lbw but he replied, 'Bullshit, I'm too far down the pitch!' In the end, he flicked one up with his foot and belted it out of the park.

As uncomfortable as it was at the time, the incident had some positive effects. The authorities outlawed underarm bowling and, as a team, we went straight to New Zealand for a series where we knew we'd hear some advice from the natives. The first one-day international was at Eden Park in Auckland and there were 42,000 people in the crowd, including heaps of guys dressed up in all-white lawn bowls gear, and people threw lawn bowls jacks out onto the field. Greg Chappell made a century, just to show how strong he was. We also lost, which was probably a good idea too!

10

The greats

I PLAYED WITH and against some of the legends of the game, and for the sake of entertainment, I've set myself the task here of picking three teams. One is the World XI, one is the Australian XI, and the third is what you might call a Fun XI—a team I'd love to play with, featuring some of the characters of the game. In all three cases, they come from the period Boxing Day 1978 to the end of March 1994, which covers my time as an Australian Test player. That means the likes of Barry Richards, Mike Procter and Graeme Pollock, the great South Africans against whom I never had the privilege of playing, miss out on my World team. Nevertheless, I'm sure it's still a strong team.

First picked in my World XI is **Sunil Gavaskar** of India. Sunny had a fabulous technique that stood him in good stead throughout his career, and a great record against the West Indies, even when they were in their pomp. He prospered at home and away, not just on flat Indian wickets. He made a poultice of runs against the West Indies at home and truckloads against Australia. If he got a start he'd inevitably get a hundred, and his record of 10,122 runs at 51.12 in Test cricket is brilliant. He's the best opener I played against.

Gordon Greenidge of the West Indies will walk out to bat with Gavaskar, chosen just ahead of Desmond Haynes, with whom he opened for the West Indies for so long. They're virtually interchangeable, Greenidge with 7558 runs at 44.72 and Haynes 7487 runs at 42.29. You could throw England's Geoff Boycott into that mix as well, with his 8114 runs at 47.72, a self-motivated guy whose critics called him selfish, but an interesting character. I enjoy his company still. He's a pleasant guy and a very astute judge of cricket. One thing I heard about Boycott is that as a young man he could virtually only play a forward defensive shot. Then, through sheer hard work and determination, he made himself into a great player. I really admire that— and don't forget that he played a lot in England, where the new ball swings and nips around, so he was right in the firing line. I was very close to throwing him in this team. England can be a great place to bat when the sun's out, but what about those days at Headingley, where Boycott grew up, when it's overcast and the new ball is moving around? It can be a nightmare.

The greats

'Dessie' Haynes was a competitor. He could be belliger-
ent, but usually he was an accumulator of runs who liked
to play against Australia, and he was a good fellow off the
field. But Greenidge could take the game away from you.
He could attack, but he had a good technique for the tough
times, too, probably developed in England, where he'd lived
from the age of 14. He got big scores against everyone,
and it's gold if you get those big runs from your top three
batsmen. He didn't play at his best in his early days against
Australia, but when I played against him I respected him
enormously. He was a prickly character—unlike Haynes,
who was bubbly and laughing all the time. Gordon had an
edge to the way he played and conducted himself, but he
could seriously bat.

It would surprise no one to see **Sir Isaac Vivian
Alexander Richards** as my No. 3 batsman. Viv is my
favourite player, although I wouldn't have said so at the
time I crossed swords with him—we were both competitive
people, and he was a major antagonist to our team. He had
the famous swagger and bravado—and all the shots, with
8540 runs at 50.23 to show for it. He considered the best
form of defence to be attack, but if he had to dig in and
defend, which wasn't all that often, he could do that, too.

If Viv had the big bats they have nowadays, I shudder
to think what he could have done. And if there are guys
in the IPL getting $2 million, what would Viv be worth?
Maybe $5 million? Viv would win games by himself

with the bat, and he'd also get a lot of wickets with those phantom off-spinners of his. When we played the West Indies back then, we'd have Malcolm Marshall, Michael Holding, Curtly Ambrose and Courtney Walsh coming at us. Then Viv would sidle up to bowl and, as a batsman, I'd be thinking, 'I've got to go here!' Your judgement can become clouded when you look at your own era, but I've watched a lot of cricket and I know Viv was special. He's still revered. I've been with him in India and in other parts of the cricketing world, and he's worshipped. When he walks into a room, everyone knows he's arrived. He has a rare presence.

In recent times, we've actually been able to sit down and chat with no pressure of looming cricket. We've talked about the good old days, and he's quite a political person as well, Viv, having been to study in Cuba. If you get him going he's well versed in global politics.

Sachin Tendulkar walks into my World XI at No. 4, even though I only played against him when he was young, back in the 1991–92 series in Australia, when he extracted two great hundreds from us. He was only 18 years old, but he'd already made his name as a wunderkind with runs against other countries—and then we got to see how good he was.

His 148 not out against us in Sydney that summer was special, but then we went to Perth, where Indian teams traditionally struggle against the unique pace and bounce, and he peeled off 114 there too, against Craig McDermott, Mike Whitney, Paul Reiffel and Merv Hughes. We won easily, but we all knew we'd witnessed the arrival of a superstar. Twenty years and 15,921 Test runs at an average of 53.78 later (and not to mention a squillion one-day international runs), he has to be in my team. Sachin was fast on his feet and small in stature, which is a bit of a theme in my World XI.

Another shorter guy to make the grade is **Brian Lara**, who bats at No. 5 in my team. Again, I didn't play a lot of cricket against him, but it was enough. I was up close when he made his famous 277 in Sydney in January 1993, in just his fifth Test match. Like Tendulkar, he'd arrived with a thunderclap. I think he'd be still batting in that match now had Carl Hooper not run him out. I'd say that Brian Lara is as close to genius as a batsman could get, and his subsequent feats bear me out. He once made 501 not out for Warwickshire. He'd been on a run of scoring hundreds in county cricket, and Ray 'Razor' Phillips, the former Queensland wicketkeeper, rang me one particular morning after Lara had finished the day's play unbeaten on 100 and said, 'What about Lara?' I replied, 'Yeah, amazing, that many hundreds in a row.' He said, 'What are you talking about? He made 500!'

I was incredulous. My best was 205, and that took about ten hours, so the game wouldn't be long enough for me to make 500. That innings against Durham at Edgbaston is the only quintuple hundred in first-class history, and he ended up breaking the Test world record with 375. Then, after Matthew Hayden took that mark from him, he bettered it again with the only 400 (not out) in Test cricket, against England at Antigua in 2004. Lara had a high backlift, which you wouldn't necessarily be teaching kids, and he had his own technique, like a lot of West Indians, yet it was solid. He was as good a player of spin bowling as you'd find, because he could really use his feet.

A lot of people tried to compare Lara (11,953 runs at 52.88) with Tendulkar, but they were quite different players. I'd say this: if you wanted someone to bat for your life, you might go for Tendulkar, but for a freakish score out of nothing, it would be Lara. He had a little more genius about him, a quirkiness, and the high end of his game was incredible. I was lucky enough to be in the West Indies to see him win a Test against Australia at Barbados in 1999 with 153 not out on the last day, an innings *Wisden* rated the second-best single Test innings ever (behind Bradman, of course!).

I went for an all-rounder at No. 6 for balance in my World XI, which leaves Javed Miandad of Pakistan missing out narrowly. I used to call Miandad 'the street-fighter'. You'd want him in the trenches with you, and sometimes he might not look too flash, but he was a workmanlike player. He had good feet and he was feisty and hard to get out. He was an outstanding player.

The greats

That No. 6 slot belongs to **Sir Ian Botham** of England in a photo finish. Generally speaking, the records of Botham, Imran Khan (Pakistan), Kapil Dev (India) and Sir Richard Hadlee (New Zealand) are quite similar, and any of them is worthy of a spot in this team. In this case, I chose Botham through intuition and personal experience rather than pure statistics, because I saw so much of him.

He was there in 1978–79 when I broke into the Australian team, and he was already an antagonist; he took wickets, made runs and created catches. He might not have been so effective against the West Indies, for instance, but he was incredible against Australia. He destroyed us in the 1981 and 1985 Ashes tours, and in 1986–87 he made a hundred in Brisbane to turn the series after England's touring team under Mike Gatting had lost to all the states in the lead-up. It took until the 1989 Ashes tour for us to get on top of Botham, but we were well overdue, and then by 1993, when we were dominant, he'd retired.

I liked playing against Beefy, and there aren't too many guys you could say would be first in your dressing room, whether he made nought or a hundred, after a day's play. A lot of us can be sulky in that situation and say, 'I'm not going in there,' but Botham left everything out on the field. He was a wonderful competitor, but there was no sledging apart from subtle stuff. His record (5200 runs at 33.54

and 383 wickets at 28.40) is superb. Then again, Imran (3807 runs at 37.69 and 362 wickets at 22.81), Hadlee (3124 runs at 27.16 and 431 wickets at 22.29) and Kapil (5248 runs at 31.05 and 434 wickets at 29.64) all made compelling cases. Imran was fast when he was young, then clever as he became older, and his batting improved over time. I give a big tick to Kapil for being a great fast bowler who's come out of the subcontinent, where the wickets offered him virtually nothing.

In the end, I didn't want Kapil or Hadlee batting at No. 6, since they were bowling all-rounders, whereas Botham and Imran could handle themselves anywhere in the top order. I was spoilt for choice, because this was a great era for all-rounders, and there's every reason why cricket has never produced many genuine all-rounders, or guys who could make the team either to bat or bowl. It's too tough to get out and bat in the top order after you've bowled your 25 overs. Jacques Kallis of the modern all-rounders tends to operate against that theory, but Kallis was a freak. Had I played against him, he might well have been in this team.

My wicketkeeper is England's **Alan Knott**, just ahead of Jeffrey Dujon of the West Indies. Knott finished with 269 dismissals and 4389 runs at 32.75, a terrific record, but oddly, he's not often mentioned these days because he left the game quietly. Knott didn't follow the usual path into television commentary or coaching, and hence people tend to forget how good he was with the gloves. In WSC and then back with the English team beyond that, he was a great competitor, and very quirky. His gear was always taped up and patched, but you could never underestimate him. He was superb up over the stumps to the spinners, even with Derek Underwood firing them in on wet tracks.

I'm sure Knott made some mistakes, but I can't remember them. And he could bat. The way he played was unusual. We couldn't work out where he was going to hit the ball; he'd take you to odd areas with quirky shots, and he even hit those lap sweeps in the days before anyone else really tried them.

Jeff Dujon was a good mate, even when the West Indies and Australia were going at it hammer and tongs. He rarely had to stand up to the stumps because they didn't usually play a spinner, but you'd see him standing back and flying around to the quicks like a gymnast. I used to think about the pounding his hands would have taken with four quick bowlers hitting them all day long, and the concentration you'd need to do his job day in, day out. He was extremely good, and whenever he contributed with the bat it would be when the West Indies were struggling. If they were 5–400 you might not expect him to get many, but if they were 5–150, he'd get some runs, guaranteed. He was one of those players and his record (272 dismissals and 3322 runs at 31.94) is really good.

Keepers, of course, have had their lot changed by Adam Gilchrist since I stopped playing. Gilchrist introduced the era where the keeper virtually has to be able to bat in the top six, or at the least get some big runs. That spawned the likes of India's M.S. Dhoni, South Africa's A.B. de Villiers and Australia's Brad Haddin, and it's great for the balance of the team.

A.B. de Villiers is another favourite of mine and I like his approach. He doesn't like the game drifting. He can drop anchor if he needs to, but generally he'll look to score, and he has a wide array of shots, although I do believe his wicketkeeping is taking percentage points off his batting. De Villiers would be a far more dominant, match-winning player if he didn't have to take the gloves. As a keeper-batsman his record is one of the best, but it's hard to bat at No. 5 or 6 as a keeper, which is a demanding job, both physically and mentally. You don't want to come off a day in the field and then put on the pads straight away.

My spinner is **Abdul Qadir** of Pakistan, just ahead of Derek Underwood. I couldn't pick Muttiah Muralitharan, because I only played a tour game against him when he was a kid, and I'm only counting Test matches, otherwise the Sri Lankan would be in the mix. But England's left-armer Underwood (297 wickets at 25.83) was seriously good, almost a medium-pacer. I played against him in the 1979–80 series, after the WSC split had been mended, and, to be honest, he wasn't as troublesome in Australia, where the pitches are harder. But he had to be respected anywhere, and on a difficult or turning wicket he was very tough to combat. On an uncovered wicket he'd have been impossible to play.

Qadir is one of the great leg-spinners, and he was a nightmare for me to play, especially in Pakistan. He'd come around the wicket to me as a left-hander, and bowl into the footmarks. He had all the deliveries, especially a brilliant wrong 'un or googly. Qadir had a bouncy way of going about the game, and he added something special. He was a character. It's strange: Underwood ran in a long way, and Qadir had this bouncing run-up, yet in modern cricket we're coaching spinners to walk up like Shane Warne did. It doesn't seem quite right to me. Why are we ruling out the longer, fluent run for spinners, like that of India's Anil Kumble or Australia's Bruce Yardley? It seems to me that when a lot of young spinners shuffle up to bowl, they don't have momentum through the crease. Sometimes coaches need to realise that when they made Shane Warne, they broke the mould. There's only one of him.

Choosing my three quick bowlers was tricky, to say the least, but I picked two West Indians, which won't surprise too many given the way they terrorised everyone in the eighties. The first is the late, great **Malcolm Marshall**, who tragically died a few years ago, far too young at the age of 41. Marshall is the number-one guy for me, an all-conditions bowler, with 376 wickets at 20.94. I respect the fact he got a lot of wickets in India, a true test of a fast bowler's character. When I played against him myself, he was the one I rated the highest, although they were all difficult.

I liked Malcolm off the field, and out in the middle I can only imagine that he'd be a captain's dream. Throw the ball to him, and he'd make something happen. His strike rate (a wicket every 46 balls in Tests) is incredible. In fact, he'd hardly bowl a spell without getting a wicket for you. It's interesting that he had a front-on action, which when I was growing up was considered a bit of a no-no for quick bowlers. The theory was that you needed to get side-on to bowl outswingers, but Marshall could do it with a late wrist release. He had a quick arm action and it was difficult to pick up his length, which effectively meant that he *felt* quicker than everyone else.

This team shapes up quite well, and the addition of **Wasim Akram**, Pakistan's magnificent left-arm quick, makes it stronger still. I didn't face Akram a lot, but I do respect his record in all conditions (414 wickets at 23.62 in Tests). Like Marshall, he had that quick arm action that made life difficult for a batsman. In Pakistan, where the ball reverses, he could be quite lethal. Then if you put him on an Australian track with the pace and bounce, he was very dangerous.

Akram was a bit different. He could go missing for a while, then come back with the old ball and he'd lift again.

The greats

In a sense he was typical of the Pakistanis, who would be unstoppable if they ever got it together as a team. When Imran played and captained, they had a period where there weren't as many dramas around the team, and they were close to the best in the world. Imran extracted the best from them, and in the era when the West Indies were so dominant, they were the closest to beating them. Akram was a big part of that.

It was virtually impossible for me to choose between two fast bowlers for the last spot in the World XI, but I've taken **Joel Garner** (259 wickets at 20.97), just ahead of Sir Curtly Ambrose (405 wickets at 20.99), probably in the end because I played more against Joel when I was younger. I played a couple of times against Curtly, who was terribly difficult to handle and actually quite similar in style to Joel. But 'Big Bird' Garner was a great, there's no doubt. He could ramp up the pace if he wanted to, and he could bowl on the line of your body and have someone at bat-pad and behind square to make it awkward. His yorker delivered from that 2-metre-plus height was brilliant, and his extra bounce made him difficult to hook. Ambrose had all the same traits, and he could bowl all day, but I only caught him at the end of my time. I'm leaving Curtly to be 12th man and handle the reggae music for the dance floor.

MY WORLD XI

Sunil Gavaskar (India)

Gordon Greenidge (West Indies)

Sir Vivian Richards (West Indies)

Sachin Tendulkar (India)

Brian Lara (West Indies)

Sir Ian Botham (England)

Alan Knott (England)

Malcolm Marshall (West Indies)

Wasim Akram (Pakistan)

Joel Garner (West Indies)

Abdul Qadir (Pakistan)

Sir Curtly Ambrose (West Indies) 12th man

MY BEST AUSTRALIAN team only includes players with whom I played at least one Test match, so the likes of Ricky Ponting and Adam Gilchrist are the obvious omissions. It's a very good side nonetheless.

I have **Matthew Hayden**, my fellow Queenslander, coming in at the top of the order. He could have come into the team a lot earlier, but when we took him to England in 1993 for the Ashes tour, Michael Slater got the nod to open the batting with Mark Taylor, and it stalled Matthew for a while. But 'Haydos' ended up with 8625 runs at 50.73 in

Test cricket, all scored at the top of the order, and that's a phenomenal record. I only played one Test with him, in South Africa in 1994, my last tour. Hayden broke his thumb and went out of the team again, but he made up for it later. People used to talk about his faulty technique, but the fact is he made a lot of runs at the Gabba, where the fast bowlers love to bowl, and he'd reel off 1000 runs in the Sheffield Shield every year.

But he took time to establish himself, because in that period from 1994 we had an exceptional team. Hayden had a hunger for runs and he loved batting, and I reckon his brother Gary would have thrown him 30,000 balls over the years. He had no fear, he enjoyed the challenge, and his technique got better over time. He knew his strengths and weaknesses. Unusually for a left-hander, he wasn't so much of a cutter, and he didn't squirt the ball to third man. He was more into whipping the ball to the on side, and driving down the ground, and he'd just bully the bowlers.

My other opener is **Mark Taylor**, just in front of Justin Langer. 'Tubby' scored 7525 runs at 43.49 at the top of the order, was a great slip fieldsman and became an outstanding captain, so he deserves his position. He arrived as a star on the 1989 Ashes tour when he made 800-plus runs. He was sturdy and dependable, with quite a few shots he played really well. He was what I call a very smart player, and that came through in the way he batted, the way he understood conditions.

If you're an opening batsman you're in the firing line. It's the engine room, right there, and Tubby performed. He would pick the line and play it; the secret is not to go fishing for the ball. If it moves off the seam, you miss, which isn't necessarily a disaster, but some guys look for terrors in the wicket. Mark Taylor didn't; they don't come much stronger.

Justin Langer showed something early and was thrown in for his debut against the West Indies in 1992–93, then hit on the helmet by Ian Bishop with the first ball he faced in Test cricket. When he extracted a half-century, we all knew he had the guts and the technique to make a very good player, although it took him some time after that to reach his best. He could easily have won a slot in my team, but I played more cricket with Taylor, which tipped the balance in his favour.

I picked **David Boon** at first drop, just in front of Ian Chappell, with whom I didn't play for very long. I have the utmost respect for Chappelli, having played with him in 1979–80 and come across his forthright views. I've had a million arguments with him, always about cricket, but I respect his thinking. You never die wondering with him, and he's worth hearing out. I learnt so much from those veteran players when I first came into the Test team.

But Boon was the salt of the earth. He was the guy you wanted coming in at the fall of the first wicket. He was our Rock of Gibraltar. Boonie came into the side in

1984 around the time I became captain; he was young and he'd made a lot of Shield runs for Tasmania, but it took time for him to develop as a Test player, eventually making 7422 runs at 43.65. For a lot of guys, it's about how you handle getting dropped, and he was one of those. He didn't sulk. He went back and worked his way into the Test team again, then once he established himself, he made important runs at the top of the order, where it's so important. Boon made runs in India, Australia and England, on three different types of pitches. If you were in the trenches and about to go over the top, you'd need Boon with you. He also became a very fine, unflinching bat-pad fieldsman. Every so often we'd tap him on the helmet to make sure he was awake, but he took stunning catches in there. He had no fear, which helped.

I want **Greg Chappell** at No. 4 for my Australian team. There's been some debate over the years about which of the Chappell brothers was best. If Greg isn't the best Australian batsman I played with, then it's a photo finish with Ricky Ponting, who might have just pipped him in my eyes. That's a pub debate for the ages, because you have to respect Ponting for his 13,378 runs, yet Greg played a lot of his career against the West Indies when they were at their marauding best, equipped with four world-class fast bowlers virtually the whole time.

Surprisingly, Greg never toured India. He played in an era when Australian teams didn't go there, and by the time we went back there in 1986 he'd retired. But his record is impeccable, with 7110 runs at 53.86. He's gone on to coach in India and run the Australian talent identification program at the NCC. He's also enjoyed success in the commercial world. He has to be in my team.

Steve Waugh's wonderful record (10,927 runs at 51.06) gets him into my Australian team at No. 5. I loved the way the 'Iceman' went about his cricket, and I played a lot with him, dating from his debut as a 20-year-old with a big reputation. He came into the side in 1985 when we were struggling, and was a thrashing machine who would play big shots to almost every ball. He had no defensive instinct at all, but through his own skill acquisition he became the complete player over time.

He was dropped twice, and he was probably played too soon because our team wasn't performing. Initially he drew confidence from success in one-day cricket, especially the 1987 World Cup when we finished on top of the world. He'd bowl at the death of those games and he was tough. Then in England in 1989, he exploded with the bat, scoring his first ton then adding more.

Steve had that last-man-standing attitude. He'd see anything through to the bitter end, and getting him out when he'd dropped anchor was hard work for bowlers. He accumulated a great batting record and he was also a handy bowler until his back and shins packed in on him. He bowled a skidding bouncer that was quite dangerous, and he had a knack of taking important wickets. I probably should have used him more in the early years, when he was fit enough to bowl. Who could forget him bowling three consecutive bouncers to Viv Richards at Brisbane in 1988–89, as a message to the West Indians that they were in for a fight?

He also became a highly successful captain, with a penchant for trying different tactics. Admittedly he had a great team—Australia was by far the best in the world in that period from 1999—but he initiated the player numbers on the shirts (something no one had thought of before; I'm No. 299 and proud of it), and he was responsible for making that baggy green cap sacred again. He was capable of thinking outside the box, Steve: 'I've got this fantastic cricket team. How do I make it even more focused? How do I make this more special?' He and John Buchanan as coach established the Australian way of playing, and a lot of what happens today comes from that period, when that 'brand' was established.

The last batting spot goes to **Mark Waugh**, Steve's twin, in a close race with Dean Jones and Doug Walters. This was a very difficult selection, made tougher by the fact that Jones is a close mate. 'Junior' Waugh (so named because he was the second of the twins to enter the world, by a factor of a minute or two) gets the nod for all-round skill and for being tougher than people realised.

I only played one season with Doug Walters, and he was brilliant, but he missed the 1981 Ashes tour when he probably should have been picked, and then he retired. He was a great bloke to have around the change rooms and he was a special talent. As for Jones, he could have played close to 100 Tests, but had to be content with 52 Tests and 3631 runs at 46.55. In the end, he was probably better known for his magnificent batting in one-day cricket, which he revolutionised with his aggressive running between wickets.

But I look at Waugh with 8029 runs at 41.81 and I factor in that he didn't worry about averages. He didn't have that ruthless streak where if he was 100, he went looking for 200. He looked for an opportunity to take the bowling down and quite often that attitude cost him his wicket. But he was a great player to watch, he had a great technique and he played the game the right way. From ball one, he played aggressively. He wanted to entertain the crowd, and he didn't like to let the game drift. On top of that, he was a brilliant fielder and he could take handy wickets with medium pace or off-spin. As a slipper, there weren't too many better, ever. Mark Taylor was excellent, if not as freakish, Michael Clarke is very good at first slip now, and Shane Warne wasn't far behind. But Junior could take blinding catches, and throw down the stumps from in close or field at bat-pad on the off side. It's a winning package.

The wicketkeeper's position was difficult. It came down to Rod Marsh or **Ian Healy**, but I've gone with Heals, having played a little more with him. Their records are quite similar (Healy 395 dismissals, Marsh 355; Healy 4356 runs at 27.39, Marsh 3633 at 26.51). What swayed me was seeing Healy keep many times to Shane Warne's bowling, standing up to the stumps on wearing wickets and tricky pitches where the ball was flying out of the foot-marks. If Heals missed a chance at those times, it would be a rarity. He had a great work ethic (not that Rod was lazy!), and he made handy runs, with gutsy innings when we needed them, in the same mould as Knott and Dujon. He played smart. He played as the game should be played. As a captain you didn't have to worry about him.

It goes virtually without saying that my spinner is **Shane Warne** (708 wickets at 25.41). It was fun to captain him, with the way he injected life into the team just doing his stuff. He never missed a beat, and things happened when he was in the game. People forget how tough it is to bowl leg-spin. They say, 'Why haven't we got more leg-spinners?' That's quite simple: it's a frightfully hard skill to master, and Warne was unique.

I also want **Dennis Lillee** (355 wickets at 23.92) in my team. The game came to life when Dennis had the ball; he was such a fierce competitor. There was no situation where Dennis thought the game was done or winding down. He'd always be in the batsman's face, then backing it up with skill. His attitude was the main thing: it was never say die. If the wicket was flat, he'd run his fingers across the ball and bowl cutters. He adapted to conditions, the way

Malcolm Marshall did later: 'Okay, I'm not going to get blokes caught at slip here, so I might look for an lbw.' He'd make those subtle variations and he'd run in all day.

Who could forget the day he knocked over Viv Richards with the last ball of the day's play in the Test match against the West Indies at the MCG in 1981? He intimidated batsmen, as did the crowd chanting, 'Lill-eee . . . Lill-eee.' You'd have to have ice in your veins to hear that and not be affected by it. I'd absolutely love to have a team with Warne and Lillee together.

Glenn McGrath is there with the new ball in my team along with Lillee. The 'Pigeon' kept it simple, but he had that never-say-die attitude common among great bowlers. Quick bowlers especially can't throw in the towel or moan about their lot in life all the time. Their first spell might be a shocker, but they have to come back and find something. McGrath is 195 centimetres tall, and he used that height, extracting a lot of bounce. It was after my retirement that he really emerged, on the 1995 tour of the West Indies when Mark Taylor's team toppled the champions from the Caribbean at last.

McGrath bowled bouncers at the West Indian tail, all the while knowing he had limited skill with the bat and would cop retribution later. His wrist release was brilliant; he'd stand the seam up and hit it; he was close to the stumps; and he hit the bat hard. The speed gun might not have hit the 150s, but he bowled a heavy ball, as they say, ending with 563 wickets at 21.64. He was his own harshest critic; if he was hit for four he'd castigate himself. He hated going for runs. He was a special breed.

The last spot in my team has a rider. If we're playing in England, I want Terry Alderman, who was an amazing bowler in that part of the world. But if the game is played in Australia, I want **Jeff Thomson**. Since we're talking here about Australia, I'm running with Thommo, with special mentions to Craig McDermott, Geoff Lawson, Bruce Reid and Merv Hughes. All those guys were wonderful to have in the side, and their records were great. Merv Hughes played down his skills sometimes, but his 212 wickets at 28.38 tell us he could bowl. McDermott had wonderful technique, Lawson was a great fast bowler, and Reid at his best was right up there.

But Thomson had that explosive factor. As a captain, you might just say, 'Jeffrey, all I want is for you to bust a few heads!' Imagine the terror he'd put into the opposition. Arguably he was the fastest bowler ever, timed with high-speed cameras at 160 km/h in a net session in 1975 and again in 1976. He didn't like batsmen, and he was incredibly athletic. We were amazed to see the stretches he'd do at warm-ups, his leg behind his neck! Of course his action was unusual, with its slinging motion coming from behind his back; whatever the speed gun was saying, you could add a few km/h for that. Batsmen could never pick him with any ease.

As for Alderman, he was born to bowl in England. He took more than 40 wickets each time on two tours of England in 1981 and 1989, and sadly missed the 1985 tour because he was on suspension for making a tour of South Africa. Clem was quick when he was young, and he could make the ball bounce from his 190 centimetres, but he's best known for his control and swing, amassing 170 wickets at 27.15. I'm giving him 12th man duties in the knowledge that when this team swings to England, he's playing.

MY AUSSIE XI

Matthew Hayden

Mark Taylor

David Boon

Greg Chappell

Steve Waugh

Mark Waugh

Ian Healy

Shane Warne

Dennis Lillee

Glenn McGrath

Jeff Thomson

Terry Alderman (12th man)

The greats

THE CONCEPT OF my Fun XI is to pick blokes whose company I enjoyed. It would be a riotous environment, with Test players who would be hard to shift from the dressing room at night and hard to wake up on day two. Remember, we're talking about blokes from before the modern era of ultra-professionalism; these guys played hard on *and* off the field.

Geoff Marsh is opening the batting, for certain. The old 'Swamp Fox' was a country bloke from Wandering in Western Australia; he loved the game, loved a beer after a day's play (when he'd be on the music machine playing the Beach Boys), and he was a fine player. He got us away to some great starts, and he was an excellent lieutenant for me. Marsh played with a smile on his face, and he had a quirky sense of humour. I'll never forget him captaining the team at Lancashire on the 1989 tour the morning after we'd won the First Test and celebrated overly hard. Talk about organised chaos!

David Boon has to be there. He was a good drinking buddy, he had great cricketing skills and he was one of the good guys. It would be hard to get out of the dressing room with him there. Boon broke Rod Marsh's Sydney–London drinking record with 52 cans in 1989, and managed to stay on his feet at the other end. He copped a stern talking-to from Simpson later, but he still made a poultice of runs on that tour.

The Fat Cat, **Greg Ritchie**, bats at No. 3 in my Fun XI. He's a very funny man, Greg, and he has a way with storytelling, doing great foreign accents. He knows how to have a good time, although he's not so much a beer-drinker—it's more likely to be a Chivas Regal for him, which used to get him into a fair bit of trouble. Out on the field he'd always be looking for the humorous anecdote, and he could be annoying but in a funny way. When Fat Cat was on a supporters' tour, he ran out onto the ground and virtually tackled Steve Waugh in the West Indies in 1995 after he'd made 200 at Jamaica. He made about a 3-metre drop over the boundary to get out there. With Fat Cat, you tend to look back and think, 'Maybe we should've got more out of his cricket,' but although he loved the game and he was skilful, it wasn't everything to him. He was mischievous, the master of disaster. If something madcap happened, you'd look around and there'd be Fat Cat.

Dean Jones is there, and he's the same sort of extrovert character as Ritchie. He can rub people up the wrong way, Deano, but I get him. His nickname was 'The Legend'. He might have thought he was a bit of a legend, but you just had to know he was joking. He was good to have in the rooms and good to have in the field, and we've always been close mates.

With **Doug Walters** in this team along with Boon, trying to escape from the post-match powwow in the rooms would be terribly difficult, given cold beers were still available. The passive smoke would have been a problem for everyone, although Doug (who used to smoke a few packets a day) went to get acupuncture and abruptly stopped smoking the darts! A lot of us smoked either regularly or socially in my time, when Benson & Hedges was the major sponsor. A representative used to drop a few cartons in the rooms or at the hotel and there'd be a scramble for them. Doug always seemed to have a cigarette in his mouth, and he'd have card games going if there was downtime, with ·the form guide for the races nearby. Needless to say, he was quite a player too.

I put **Rod Marsh** in as the keeper, batting a bit high at No. 6, but he's the sergeant major in all this, leading the attack, making sure the beer's cold, and probably complaining about Geoff Marsh's music.

Tim May is our spinner. He has a quirky sense of humour and he loves a good time—he's a piss-taker of the highest order.

Merv Hughes was the serial pest but he makes my team. I'm not sure how we'd control him in those circumstances, with all those characters there. Merv is full on, a captain's dream with the ball in his hand, and he was an enforcer type who made life uncomfortable for the batsmen. He'd be 100 per cent switched on when you were on the park, but take the ball out of his hand and he was the village idiot. He plays that role so well and he's happy for people to believe it, even though he's a very smart guy. If he got on a roll he'd tell stories and jokes for hours about anything; he had an incredibly retentive memory for yarns—all he needed was a cue. That makes him a must-have.

Carl Rackemann, the big 'Mocka', can bowl for this team. He's as dry as you like, a wonderful storyteller and an intelligent bloke. The farmer comes out in him often, and he used to like a drink and a smoke.

Another Queenslander, **Jeff Thomson**, would have to be there, and Thommo would hold his own in the rooms. He's a great bloke, another good storyteller, and he'd keep guys in check because he never minces his words: if he doesn't like something, he'll say so. He was also a good tourist.

Jim Higgs can be the extra spinner in the team, a guy who's very quirky and very funny. We might have to carry 'Higgsy' out at midnight, because I'm not sure he'd handle the pace with the others, but he loved a drink and a chat, and he could take the mickey out of anyone.

Bruce Yardley and Simon 'Scuba' O'Donnell get special mentions, along with Rodney Hogg, who's not a big drinker but is funny. Scuba would lead the singing; his go-to song was 'Billy Don't Be a Hero', and he was good fun in a dressing room.

Overall, it's not a bad team for a good time. Whether they'd come up for a full five-day game is questionable, though.

MY FUN XI

Geoff Marsh

David Boon

Greg Ritchie

Dean Jones

Doug Walters

Rod Marsh

Tim May

Merv Hughes

Jeff Thomson

Carl Rackemann

Jim Higgs

Rodney Hogg (12th man)

Epilogue

I LOVE MY CRICKET. The game is in my DNA, that's for sure. Whatever I've done since I retired from playing for Queensland in 1996, my life has always seemed to turn back to cricket. That's just the way it is.

So when Stuart Law approached me to be part of the Brisbane Heat's set-up for the Big Bash League recently, I jumped at the chance. Stuart and I played in Queensland's first-ever Sheffield Shield triumph in 1994–95, so we go way back. And I'd already been involved in the Heat as a director, as well as on the board of Queensland Cricket. I'm now working with the team as a sort of mentor, working with players one on one and helping Stuart, the head coach, with some of the day-to-day issues. It's more of a pure cricket role, which I know I'll enjoy. I've always loved being around teams, even after I finished playing.

The timing is appropriate, I guess, because March 2015 is the 20-year anniversary of Queensland's victory over South Australia in the Sheffield Shield final, when we broke one of the biggest hoodoos in all of world sport. Until that point, Queensland had played in the competition for 68 years without winning the title, we'd become the butt of cruel jokes and all we could do was cop it. But it was Stuart Law who lifted Lord Sheffield's trophy in March 1995, and that's a week none of us will ever forget. Since then, Queensland victories have become commonplace, and I hope we might celebrate a Big Bash League title for the Heat this summer as we prepare for that 20-year reunion.

Of course, I never played Twenty20 cricket, but I like it for what it is. In my era, the 50-over game was the popular shorter form, both at domestic and international level, and we played truckloads of it. Apart from a couple of tournaments in Hong Kong, we didn't experience much of the even shorter form. I've seen the Big Bash League, for instance, grow out of a state-based league into a hugely popular, franchise-based competition with teams in all the bigger Australian cities. I see such competitions as important to the overall game of cricket, because of the new fans they attract. The Big Bash League, now in its fourth year, has been an amazing success story, and I love seeing people who've probably never been to a live cricket match before—mums, dads and kids—really enjoying themselves.

Epilogue

As I write, Australia is the No. 2 Test nation on the ICC's rankings, just behind South Africa, having climbed to No. 1 in May 2014 under Michael Clarke's captaincy before being displaced by South Africa during a quiet period for our players over the winter. When Australia reached the No. 1 spot, it was the first time in five years we'd held the mantle, after a tough period during which Clarke's team slid to a distant No. 5 on the ICC table. As I write, Australia also holds the No. 1 ranking in 50-over cricket, with a World Cup approaching, and it feels like Australian cricket is back where it ought to be. The No. 1 Test ranking is within touching distance.

When I left international cricket in 1994, the West Indies were still the kings of the game, and we'd endured a long and fruitless struggle to overcome them. In all my time, we never defeated the West Indies in a Test series, but almost as soon as I retired, Mark Taylor's team won a Test series in the Caribbean in 1995 and ascended to No. 1 in the world, a title Australia held for a decade. In that ten-year period, Australia rarely lost a series in Test cricket, other than on the subcontinent, and won three World Cups in one-day international cricket. Although I was on the other side of the fence, I'm proud of having contributed towards making the team competitive again, and of having won three Ashes series. I can always remember Ian Chappell saying, 'Lose to whoever, but make sure it's not to England!' There's a bit of truth in that.

After falling off their perch in the Ashes loss to England in 2005, the Australian team certainly went through some difficult times. There'll always be a point when you have an ageing team while the opposition has happened upon two or three brilliant players, and the tables can turn. But in Australia we tend to expect and demand that our team stay around the No. 1 mark, and we have the advantage of our system to fall back upon. That's precisely as it should be.

Looking back

DENE BORDER

Upon learning who my father is, people often ask me, 'What's it like to be the son of Allan Border/a legend/ someone famous?' Such a vague question can't be answered simply, at least not in a way that offers any real insight. Normally I run with an easy, 'No complaints,' or, 'More pros than cons,' but rarely does casual conversation allow for a more thorough explanation of what it's like to be the son of a national icon generally, or my dad specifically.

Dad was retired from international cricket before my tenth birthday, an age when I was only just beginning to comprehend the significance of being the Australian cricket captain. As with most children, I had no real frame of reference for anything outside my own experiences, so I thought very little about how my situation might be different from that of other kids. While very young, I had a notion that

I'd follow in Dad's footsteps, not out of a desire to play international cricket but simply because that's what he did, much as the son of a doctor might initially aspire to go into medicine. Obviously I learnt as I grew up that this isn't how it works, but like any youngster playing junior cricket I still hoped to one day represent my country.

You'd think that this ambition, combined with my heritage, might have resulted in extra pressure on my game, but that was never the case. I think Dad was more cognisant of the shadow his achievements in the game might cast over me than I ever was. He was so conscious of the potential distraction that he perhaps didn't see me play as much as either of us would have liked, although he still made the effort when he could, usually trying to watch from some-where inconspicuous. While I honestly think I'd have coped with the pressures of more attention in terms of coaching and attendance, Dad's efforts most certainly prevented me from feeling any undue expectation and allowed me to get on with just enjoying the game.

But while I credit Dad with removing some of the weight from my shoulders, there's a much simpler expla-nation for why I never felt burdened by his name—I just wasn't good enough. While I did make some local junior rep teams, I was always way off the pace for higher honours, and by my mid-teens I'd acknowledged that unless I found a true hunger to pursue it, the dream of wearing the baggy green was beyond my talents. Had

I reached the level of guys like Shaun Marsh or Alister McDermott, I think I might have felt the pressure to emulate my father more keenly.

It was around those teenage years that kids took up that other art of cricket: sledging. While most let it slide—or focused on one or another of my many technical shortcomings—inevitably the odd opponent would settle on a comparison between me and my father. It caused me very little concern, and ignoring the jibes or replying with only a smile usually worked, until one day I discovered something even more effective. Playing fourth grade for Mosman in an away game, I found myself batting on a hot day chasing down a fairly modest total. Their opening young quick had a bit of fire in the belly and when I got off the mark by inelegantly spooning a drive over point for two, he felt the need to explain to me: 'You're not nearly as good as your old man.' Now perhaps it was the heat or the game situation or the fact that his look annoyed me, but this time I felt compelled to acknowledge the barb and retorted with, 'No shit, mate. If I was, I wouldn't have to play against fuckwits like you in a shithole like this.' It might not have been Shakespeare, but it did amuse his own teammates, and it created a blueprint for dealing with similar sledges in the future. The cherry on top was winning the game with a cover-driven four off his bowling and a cheeky, 'How do you like them apples?'

Obviously, Dad was something of an absentee father during his playing career, but I recognise that in hindsight—I never noticed it at the time, and it never had an effect on me as a child. It was all I knew: when he was away we didn't see him and when he was home we had plenty of time with him. I think this possibly works better than a father who lives at home but works impossibly long hours and finds it difficult to make time for the kids. Without a shred of doubt, this is largely down to our incredible mother, Jane, who held the fort when Dad was travelling. The WAGs of today have a little more opportunity to travel with the team, partly due to the increased financial capability of the players but also because the administration acknowledges the impact time away can have on some families and caters for it. This was less of a concern in Dad's era, and having such a strong woman looking after his home and family undoubtedly helped him maintain the mental capacity required to achieve at the highest level for such a long time.

Dad didn't have to endure every trip away without the family, though. When I was a young child, Mum took me and later my sister Nicole on a couple of trips with Dad, but the first one I have any memory of was the Austral-Asia Cup in Sharjah in the early part of 1990. The next was the 1993 Ashes tour, when I was nine, which saw Mum, me, Nicole and baby Tara set up home in Essex for the English summer. My celebrity at Hutton County Primary

School had less to do with my father's Test captaincy than the novelty of being an Australian classmate. It's from this trip that I have my best memories of being in the Australian dressing room. When Australia played a tour match against Essex, I was invited to be an unofficial 12th man, dressing up in full whites. Two memories stand out brightest, the first being when my favourite player, Michael Slater, took me out to the nets for a hit fresh from bagging a first-class pair. Considering other failures with the bat have seen him attempt to flush his gear down the dressing-room dunny, this highlights just how special that was! The other was being both victim and accomplice for a practical joke on the part of that perennial pest Merv Hughes. Picking up a cream bun served at tea, he took a bite and declared the cream to be off, proffering the offending treat to me to smell. My curiosity was rewarded with two nostrils full of dairy product as he rammed the perfectly fresh bun into my face. But the kicker was being coerced into paying the joke forward on the moustachioed David Boon. Merv certainly enjoyed the results more than the Keg on Legs!

During Dad's playing days I might have been a little bolder, given kids can be oblivious to their surroundings, although I was more focused on adding to my beer-bottle-top collection (the Aussie dressing room was a goldmine in those days) or picking up new words my mum was likely none too pleased about.

Another instance when Mum might not have appreciated what I learnt in the sheds was in the wake of Queensland's historic Sheffield Shield win in the 1994–95 season. I was just shy of my 11th birthday, but in the celebrations afterwards I found myself unsupervised with a few other young lads in the rooms and managed to sample some of the sponsor's product: XXXX. I think we sprayed around more than we drank, but Mum still wasn't nominating Dad for Father of the Year after that. In later years, during Dad's time as coach of Australia A and as a national selector, I tried to blend into the background whenever possible. Engaging with the public is part of the modern sportsman's job and something they generally enjoy, but the sanctum of the dressing room is a place to escape, and regardless of how warmly the team accepted my presence, I did feel like an interloper at times. I can remember agonising over just how to refer to players: Mr Hayden was too formal, while 'Haydos' felt like it should only be used by people who knew him well or didn't know him at all. And no one seemed to call anyone by their first name! Quite a few players, including Matt, would always go out of their way to make me feel comfortable.

Getting to know some of these legends of the game is another benefit of being my father's son. I've always loved chatting to the players or simply observing how they go about preparing for a game, getting an insight into their personalities and their views on the sport. It's also refreshing to know that these heroes are just regular people. I once went with Dad to Shane Warne's place, where he showed off his new surround-sound television set-up, demonstrating its capabilities by blasting out the opening scene of *Top Gun* and part of *Happy Gilmore*. That I was sitting with the then greatest run-scorer and the eventual greatest wicket-taker in Test cricket was irrelevant—it was just one Aussie bloke showing off his new gadget to another.

Like everyone else, these elite sportsmen have their worries and insecurities. I travelled with Dad when he was coaching Australia A and he and the selection panel had called up Andrew Symonds to replace the injured Shane Watson for the 2003 World Cup side. It was a somewhat controversial call at the time, given Watson's Australia A teammate Greg Blewett was in much better form. Later that night I was part of a frank conversation with the pair in which Andrew expressed some guilt at being picked ahead of Greg—who was disappointed but bore Symonds no ill will—and it was agreed that the best thing was to take the opportunity and be successful. With the team in trouble at 4–86 in the opening game against Pakistan, Andrew smashed 143 not out to set up Australia's successful defence as the world champions, doing his country—and Greg Blewett—proud.

My parentage has brought me other benefits, too. Possibly the most important for me has been my current place of employment, Macquarie Bank. Through cricket circles, my old man was friends with Guy Reynolds, who in those days headed up the foreign-exchange team at the bank. Hearing that I'd done well at school, Guy offered me a summer internship with his desk. I had little interest in finance at the time, so I initially spurned the opportunity, but when he offered me the chance again the following year, I decided to give it a go. That summer placing became a full-time role, and I still work on that same team trading currencies. An accusation of nepotism or cronyism would be warranted, given I have no formal qualification for the role, a fact of which I've been conscious throughout my career, but I've seen applicants who are better qualified on paper come and go because they just weren't suited to the role. There's no denying, though, that I would never have had the opportunity had I applied for an advertised position and not been my father's son. The best we Border children can do is try to make it on our own without seeking to trade unfairly on our family name.

The only time I really feel uncomfortable about the connection is when others use it as currency. Sometimes this is as blatant as wanting me to ask my old man for an appearance or auction item. Most are respectful, and if the request is reasonable I'll pass it on to Dad, usually while stressing heavily that it's completely without obligation. Other times people can be a little pushier, and it definitely rankles with me when they're too eager or ask me to make additional demands of Dad. I know people want to maximise these opportunities, but when such things are organised through me, people often try to get more for less, abusing their connection with me. Dad regularly gives his time up for far less than I imagine the going rate would be, so I really don't enjoy being the middleman for these types of arrangements.

Another thing that happens fairly regularly is being introduced to people as 'Allan Border's son', to which I've developed the habit of chiming in with, 'Or you can just call me Dene.' It's not that I care about people knowing who my father is, or that I'm especially worried about having an identity outside of being my father's son. It's just that it's often said with no thought to following up with my name or how we know one another. Of course, for most people I meet casually, it's the most interesting thing about me, and it's also something they remember. I once met the prime minister of the time, John Howard, while trying to stay out of the way in a corner of the Australian dressing room. We chatted rather briefly about my upcoming final year of school and my future plans. A few months later he was meeting a group of school captains in Brisbane and, recognising the Brisbane Boys' College uniform, asked how Dene Border was doing, much to the shock of my school captain.

I've had my photograph taken and even signed autographs for cricket tragics once they discovered my parentage. Watching a Test match in India, I sat in the general stands, and when word got out who my father was I garnered a stack of new friends. I always stress that I'm not the famous one, but that doesn't seem to matter to people who want even the tiniest brush with fame. Dad is pretty accessible as far as celebrities go—at that same Test in India I saw many former greats allowing people to pose next to them for a photo, but they'd do it all while continuing with their phone call and not acknowledging the fan's presence. Dad might not stop for every person who wants a photo or autograph, but at least when he does so he gives them his undivided attention.

Sometimes this recognition can be an unexpected positive, and can happen in the most unlikely of places. My sister Tara competed in aerobics and represented Australia at an international meet in Russia. As each competitor went on stage to perform, their name was displayed for the spectators. Usually you'd expect the Border name to go unrecognised in a small town outside Moscow, but the Indian team members were very excited when they discovered the link. When they realised that Tara's proud father had made the long trip to watch, they couldn't believe their luck, and it gave some common ground for the Australian and Indian teams to mix in a place they might otherwise have never really spoken.

Having said all that, I never try to distance myself from Dad's fame too much. I'm as big a cricket fan as any. Dad is certainly a hero, and I'll happily discuss at length his achievements or any other aspect of the game. I love reading articles and watching videos about cricket in Dad's era. I especially enjoy talking to him about the game and getting the inside scoop from someone who's been there and done that. The vast majority of our conversations inevitably turn to cricket, and we cover every topic under the sun, from players to administrators, and specific matches past and present to the general health of the game. I love talking cricket with anyone and everyone, but Dad most of all.

One conversation we had, however, neither of us enjoyed at all. While I was living in Sydney, Dad would make a point of catching up every time he was in town, but one night in 2009 I could tell something was amiss. Sadly, his youngest brother, Brett, had just been diagnosed with inoperable lung cancer, and we didn't know how much time he'd have left. Although I was 12 when Dad's parents passed away within a month of one another, I have no clear recollection of how Dad was at the time. Regardless, I don't think that would have been as tough as dealing with this news, given Brett had only just turned 47. Of course, Dad put a brave face on it, but he was evidently battling with the shock of it all, and we reflected on the same things anyone does when getting such upsetting news. Given the diagnosis, we agreed that all we could do was enjoy the time we had left with Brett, which Dad duly did, going on a trip with him to the 2010 Masters and playing with him on famous courses such as Pebble Beach while Brett still could. When Brett did pass away, the family made a conscious decision not to wallow in the sadness of it and chose instead to celebrate his memory with an annual trip to Nambucca Heads on the New South Wales coast. Far from being a sombre occasion, it's full of fun and precisely how Brett lived his life. I looked forward to it each year and I hope to see the tradition continue for many years to come.

I really enjoy travel, and the foundations of that passion were undoubtedly laid by the trips we did as a young family during Dad's playing career. We never got to some of the more exotic Test arenas in India or the Caribbean, but there was that trip to Sharjah and tours of the United Kingdom. In 1993, when the family was settled in Essex, Mum took my sisters and me on a great trip around Britain and Ireland. In 1995, Dad, having recently retired, was on hand to see Mark Taylor's Australian team win a historic series in the West Indies. He linked up with the rest of us afterwards for a magnificent round-the-world holiday culminating in Zimbabwe. Here we enjoyed one of the more unusual benefits of Dad's celebrity. Upon landing at the airport servicing Hwange National Park in the country's north-west, we were greeted by a ranger who was an elephant expert in the park—and a huge cricket fan. When he'd heard Dad was to be a guest, he decided to pick us up personally. The truly amazing part, however, was when he detoured on the way back to the game lodge to find a herd of elephants. These giant animals were milling about the vehicle within touching distance, and we could gently lob acacia pods to them, an experience not usually available to a tourist. It was a massive highlight of an already memorable trip.

Nicole and I followed Dad to Zimbabwe the following year, when he got involved with the World Wildlife Fund to play exhibition games to raise money and awareness for the plight of the black rhino. A Channel Seven crew tagged along, and Dad leveraged his involvement to have his elder children on board. The highlight this time was in Matusadona National Park on the shores of Lake Kariba, where we were introduced to an adolescent female rhinoceros, Chewore, who had grown up semi-wild under the 24-hour surveillance of armed rangers. Not many people can claim to have patted one of these amazing creatures. Later on we saw Chewore having a mud bath and bounding out of the water like an enormous puppy to frolic with the rangers as she had when she was a baby. But she now weighed a few hundred kilos and was more difficult to control. She soon turned her attention to the small group of tourists with whom we were standing. The group parted like the Red Sea, leaving Nicole to cop the attention of Chewore, who was simply out to play. When Chewore knocked her over, Nicole suffered more from shock than anything, with Chewore standing over her not sure what had gone wrong. It must have been a fun call for Dad to make home to Mum that day: 'Oh, and Nicole was bowled over by a 600-kilogram rhino.' But the best part was that the ever-attentive cameraman had caught it on tape. I've revelled in playing it back many times over the years, often in slow motion. I swear you can hear Dad chuckling in the background!

A few other trips I've taken just with Dad. Some of those have been in Australia, while he fulfilled various cricketing roles—coach, selector or commentator. The absolute highlight of these cricketing trips was undoubtedly the Adelaide Ashes Test in 1998–99. While Dad was in the commentary box, he organised for me to sit in the beautiful old scoreboard, which was an absolute dream for a cricket-mad teenager. I was put in charge of ticking over the batsmen's scores, looking through a gap straight down the wicket. It was a very special experience indeed, and I even got to chalk up my hero Michael Slater's second-innings ton. I had the big number '1' ready to go from quite a way out—the sort of jinx that would ordinarily give me nightmares—but perhaps this time it was the key, given his notorious battles with the 'nervous nineties'.

Another incredible trip with Dad was walking the Kokoda Track for Anzac Day and my 21st birthday in 2005. It's a fantastic thing to do at any point in your life—not just for the physical effort, but to get to know more about that crucial Australian campaign—and it was very special to share it with Dad. There was plenty of introspection and reflection, but one of my favourite memories comes from the long, tough first day when we were battling a particularly difficult uphill section. I pointed out an exotic-looking caterpillar right in the middle of the trail for Dad to avoid and a second later it was churned into the mud beneath his boot to my howls of protest. 'We're not here for fucking caterpillars!' came the gruff rejoinder. I'm not sure if it's the memory or his embarrassment when I tell the story that I love best!

Most recently, I took some annual leave from my job in Singapore to jump across for the 2013 Australia versus India Test match in Hyderabad. In a series we lost 4–0, it was probably the most crushing of the losses, but the silver lining was a final day to see the city. Dad was originally going to catch an early flight home, but decided to stay on and spend the day with me. By his own admission, he hasn't done too much tourist stuff in India, despite his many trips there, apart from team visits to iconic locations like the Taj Mahal. He was a little nervous about how he'd go among the cricket-mad Indian public, but he was pretty anonymous and we had a terrific day. I don't envy him having to be wary of being mobbed by fans when he travels in a place like India, but hopefully the experience will encourage him to get out and have more of a look around next time.

That problem of rarely being anonymous is one Dad has become used to and deals with well, but it must also be a strange one for someone who's otherwise a very normal bloke. He prefers a steak in a pub watching the footy to a ritzy meal in a fancy restaurant served with what he calls 'camouflage'. And he's more at home in the garden in shorts and T-shirt under a wide-brim straw hat than he is out and about in a suit and tie. This everyday behaviour also makes him a pretty typical father when you cut the cricket and fame out of the equation. His humour fits very firmly into the 'Dad jokes' stereotype; his favourites when we were young were saying, 'You spilled something on your shirt,' then, when we looked down, flicking our nose; and—to Mum's continual disgust—'Quick, quick, pull my finger!' Like many dads, he's comfortable trying to embarrass his daughters and also somewhat uncomfortable with technology, despite his best efforts. These things combined on a family trip to Noosa, when my sister spotted someone from Brisbane she knew but was trying to avoid. Dad thought it would be hilarious to embarrass Nicole by slyly sending her a couple of texts pretending he was that person and had seen her fobbing him off. His carefully thought-out plan was foiled, of course, when the texts all appeared in her phone as from 'Dad'.

Perhaps because he followed his boyhood dream to fruition alongside characters like Merv Hughes, this kind of immature fun is a big part of the private Allan Border. It does mean he can be a real pest, never including himself in a family game of Trivial Pursuit but still yelling out the occasional answer he knows from the couch in front of the television. Or calling using a pseudonym even though you know it's him every time. Some of that behaviour must have rubbed off on me, as any time the family goes out to dinner, Mum insists that Dad and I can't sit next to one another. But while his antics sometimes have us laughing with him, we enjoy even more the chances we get to laugh *at* him. In the family they're known as 'Dadisms', and I think the best example is told by my little brother and sister. On a trip to the Caribbean in 2008, while Dad was a Cricket Australia director, Lachy and Tara were sitting with him at the breakfast table when Mum returned from the hotel buffet complaining that she'd had to use a tiny teaspoon to scoop out her muesli because someone had taken the ladle provided. Eyes turned to Dad, who paused halfway through lifting a giant spoon from his bowl to his mouth! He was so embarrassed he gently wrapped the offending utensil into a napkin so he could be gone before anyone else saw it.

As I get older and see more of the world, I become increasingly grateful for what I have, and in particular my parents. Growing up, I think most kids take their circumstances for granted, regardless of their situation, but probably more so when they're comfortable. It's a win in the lottery of birth just to be born somewhere with basic human rights like access to clean water, housing and an education. But to also be blessed with a devoted, loving family is something I consider fortunate on a daily basis. And while I can only credit the former to my own parents' win in the birth lottery, the latter is definitely something for which they deserve full credit. So all the benefits of being the son of a famous father aside, I'm simply thankful to have as my parents two very good people who've made sacrifices and worked hard to give me every opportunity in life. Mum hasn't got enough attention from me here, but she's a truly wonderful woman who had to do most of the day-to-day parenting alone. And Dad is widely championed as the epitome of mental fortitude and working to make the most of your abilities, as well as simply being a good bloke. So that's the real answer to what it's like to be the son of Allan Border: that I've had a terrific upbringing from a man I admire as a person first, a father second and a cricketer a distant third.

But if someone asks me tomorrow, I'll probably just say, 'No complaints. More pros than cons.'

Acknowledgements

I AM INDEBTED to many people for their help in the production of this book—Octagon for planting the seed, Allen & Unwin for getting it all together and finally to Martin Blake, journalist and friend, for putting all my thoughts down in some readable form.

About A.B.

ALLAN BORDER AO is one of Australia's most respected former cricketers. A top-order batsman, Border was the Australian captain from 1984 to 1994, overseeing the development of the Australian team from the tumultuous birth of World Series Cricket to becoming the world's most dominant team in the 1990s. He played 156 Test matches in his career, a record until it was passed by Steve Waugh. Border still holds the world record for the number of consecutive Test appearances. His world record 11,174 Test runs, including 27 centuries, was only passed by the brilliant Brian Lara in 2005. The Allan Border medal, named in his honour, is awarded annually to the most outstanding cricketer of the preceding season, and he was one of the 55 inaugural inductees of the ICC Cricket Hall of Fame.